STATELESS

ONE MAN'S STRUGGLE FOR AN IDENTITY

GERARD VAN LEEUWEN

Author: Gerard van Leeuwen

Translation: Leonie Gerritsen

Editing: Kate McDonnell

Publisher: Amsterdam Publishers

ISBN 13 (ebook): 978-9492371324

ISBN 13 (paperback): 978-9492371317

Copyright text © Gerard van Leeuwen, 2017

www.gerardvanleeuwen.com

To Kamal

But every man is more than just himself, he also represents the unique, the very special and always significant and remarkable point at which the world's phenomena intersect, only once in this way and never again. That is why every man's story is important, eternal, sacred; that is why every man, as long as he lives and fulfills the will of nature, is wondrous, and worthy of every consideration.

Hermann Hesse, *Demian* (1919)

Kamal Kojadin

CONTENTS

2011, SARAJEVO, PROLOGUE

His gait as he walked from the long shopping street told me he had lived a hard life. I knew instinctively he was the man I had an appointment with, even though we had never met before. We had arranged to meet on the plaza in front of the Sacred Heart Cathedral in Stari Grad, the oldest part of the city. He was wearing a smart black jacket and carried a briefcase under his arm, as though this were a business meeting. I got up and walked towards him.

'Kamal?'

The man in front of me with a smile on his lined face was indeed Kamal Kojadin. Later he would say fate had brought us together there.

I was in Sarajevo to visit some humanitarian projects I was involved with. My contact, Ingrid, was a German social worker. She arranged for me to visit orphanages and homes for disabled people. Between these visits, I discovered areas of the city one would not normally stumble upon. The yet-to-be-demolished ruins that the war had left in its wake. The boarded-up buildings that housed Roma families. The packs of stray dogs entering those same buildings through the gaps between planks. The grey concrete neighbourhoods where the blocks of flats were screaming for a new layer of plaster to cover up the bullet holes still visible in the walls.

It was Ingrid who had told me about Kamal and how she had found him, a beggar living in one of the abandoned buildings. She asked me to do her a favour and meet up with him. He was lonely, liked talking to others, and would appreciate a conversation.

∾

The night before my meeting with Kamal on the plaza, Ingrid told me about her unforgettable experience in the autumn of 2010. Her husband Alija had brought in a blue envelope from the mailbox. The letter came from an organization in Travnik. Her eyes had eagerly run over the page. Ingrid had sent applications for citizenship in Kamal Kojadin's name before and she had been counting on another rejection. It said '...we have processed your appeal and approved the registration of birth retroactively. Our decision is final'. Ingrid and Alija had danced for joy, then jumped on to their motorbike and raced to see Kamal to celebrate his first day as a citizen of Bosnia-Herzegovina. He had been waiting for this day his entire life.

∾

Kamal entered Yugoslavia, his country of birth, in 1976. For years he had not been able to obtain citizenship of Yugoslavia or any of the states that had formed after the breakup of that country. The reason was simple. After his birth in Zagreb in 1944, he had not been registered at the Civil Status office. This oversight had convicted him to the life of a stateless person. No country, no organization, no person had ever needed to be responsible for him and this lack of identification, of valid documents, had marked his life. Just as other people get a stamp in their passport at a border crossing, it was as if Kamal Kojadin had been stamped 'NOBODY' at birth.

Now here I sat, at the request of a German project coordinator I barely knew, on a plaza in the heart of Sarajevo opposite a man I did not know. A man with a story. He asked me which language I preferred to use: Bosnian, French, German, English, Arabic or Italian. That alone surprised me, and I immediately became aware of my own prejudices. A beggar, six languages? Kamal spoke slowly, a mixture of French and English with a slight Arabic accent. He would often gaze at the sky or the ground as he searched for the right words. He seemed to be digging them up, the way an archaeologist would carefully lay bare a buried object. He told me how hard Ingrid had worked for him and that she had succeeded in something he had not been able to achieve all those years; she had given him official confirmation of his existence.

The story of his life was a puzzle in which the pieces were falsified papers, arrests, reluctant organizations, attempts to flee, small lies, big lies, prejudice and bureaucracy. It was also a story of a man pushed inexorably onwards by history. From Zagreb to Rome at the end of the Second World War, when he was just a baby. Then from Rome to Cairo with his parents, along an escape route the Nazis had used at the end of the war with help from the Vatican. From Cairo to Beirut via Damascus after the Egyptian Revolution. Then by way of Lausanne to Opatija in Yugoslavia. During the war there in the early nineties, he moved from Belgrade to Bihac, as the son of a Croatian fascist, and finally ended up in Sarajevo, where he sank to the status of a beggar.

It was a conversation I could not let go. As he told me his story he proudly showed me his newly acquired ID card. I took out my camera and asked if I could take a few pictures. Some weeks later, back at home, I took another look at those pictures of Kamal on the plaza. His ID card caught my eye and I zoomed in. The number on the card was 000001.

1976, LAUSANNE

He should have gone to the police, but Kamal only realised this afterwards. Instead, he had stayed at his hotel, waiting. Life is determined by chances, especially those not taken. This misjudgement had split his life in two and sealed his fate; before and after Switzerland. He would often look back to this decision that had, in his eyes, been the defining mistake of his life.

He had travelled to Lausanne to bury his father, only to find that the firm where his father had worked for so many years had already done so without informing him. The message about his father's death had reached him in Damascus. He did not have the necessary documents to allow him to travel to Switzerland. Obtaining a visa at the Swiss embassy had proved troublesome, and had taken several days. Afterwards he realised his father's superiors had been responsible for the delay in an attempt to gain time, to manipulate the situation. Four days after his father's death he had acquired a laissez-passer that allowed him to fly to Budapest and on to Zurich. From there he took the train to Lausanne. By the time he arrived all he could do was put flowers on the grave.

Only a year earlier he had been living with his father in Beirut. The civil war in Lebanon started in April 1975 with an attack on Pierre Gemayel, the leader of the Phalangists. The city was not safe anymore. Kamal Kojadin and his father Saïm lived in one of the firm's apartments near the port, which was still considered a safe area. Yet through their windows they could hear the gunfire and see the clouds of smoke over the city. They saw men being arrested and tortured by being dragged through the streets behind cars.

For almost twenty years, his father had been working at the firm Najjar & Sons, a successful trading company which did business with several countries. It was one of the many companies involved in import and export in the flourishing city of Beirut, which was the gateway to the Arab world in the sixties and seventies.

That fall the director Radjar Najjar spoke to Kamal's father. 'The situation here in Lebanon is going to get more and more difficult. We cannot keep doing business this way. We are going to open a branch in Switzerland, in Lausanne, which will become our main office in time.'

The conversation was short and to the point. The director had never needed many words to make himself clear. Then Najjar gave Kamal's father a choice. 'Would you like to work for us over there or would you prefer to leave? In that case I will pay you your pension.'

'I can't decide that right now, I understand what you're asking me, but I shall have to discuss this with my son first,' Saïm Kojadin had answered.

That same day, late in the afternoon, Kamal had seen his father come home gloomy and fatigued from his day at work. On other days Saïm would be silent, needing time to recover. This time, though, he told Kamal about his conversation with Najjar as soon as he walked in. By then his father had become fully aware of the mounting danger in Beirut. Yet he recoiled from the decision he had been asked to make. Usually Kamal was not so resolute, but he was worried about his father's health, so he said, 'It's a wonderful opportunity to go to Europe, you should do it. You'll be able to work there and find a good doctor.'

Saïm had been diagnosed with a slow-growing tumour and had mentioned before that he wished to be treated abroad. Many Lebanese went to the United States for medical care. Saïm, too, hoped to extend his life by a few years with good treatment.

'Go to Switzerland and if you find a way for me to come over, I will come,' Kamal said. He did not have a valid passport to enter the country and he knew this was preventing his father from making his decision. They would have to spend some time apart. Kamal could count on his father. Once he was there, Saïm would be able to arrange something for him. He had managed to acquire papers before, through the firm.

'I'd rather you didn't stay in Beirut. You must go somewhere safe, Kamal.'

∽

On 11 January 1976 Kamal said goodbye to his father in a garage somewhere in a suburb of Beirut. Kamal left by car with a few others heading for the Syrian capital Damascus. He anxiously embraced his father, not realising that this would be their last embrace. It was going to be a dangerous journey through an area controlled by militia groups with roadblocks. A few days later, his father would fly to Switzerland.

'Call me as soon as you can,' Saïm said. 'Or call the firm and leave a number if you can't reach me.'

Two days after reaching Lausanne, Kamal called him. 'I'm still tired from travelling and I'm finding the work very hard. I need you here and I have an appointment at the UNHCR office tomorrow to see what I can arrange for you.'

'Why UNHCR, isn't that for refugees? Can't Najjar do anything? They arranged your papers too, didn't they?'

'The firm won't cooperate, I don't know why. They won't tell me who their contacts are, maybe to protect them. They're acting strangely, as if it doesn't interest them. They've also already got somebody to replace me.'

Everyone at the firm knew Saïm Kojadin wouldn't live for much longer. He was becoming more and more unwell and less able to do his job. Old Najjar's children had taken over the management of the firm during the move to Lausanne. His son and daughter owned the company now. The daughter's husband had become particularly influential. He had no interest in a sick old man who had been his father-in-law's loyal right hand for years. To him Kojadin was probably just a financial burden, who did not perform well anymore and was also entitled to a hefty pension. He was owed a single payment of nineteen times his monthly salary, three thousand Swiss francs at the time, making almost sixty thousand francs in total. The firm would benefit if no heir came forward to claim the money after Saïm's death. Kamal later found out that the son-in-law had used his contacts to make sure the Swiss embassy in Damascus delayed granting him permission to travel to Switzerland.

For months Kamal waited in Damascus, hoping to be reunited with his father. Rather than the good news he hoped for, however, on 27 September he received word that his father, Saïm Kojadin, had died.

∼

By the time he got to Lausanne, he quickly discovered that everything he had wanted to do as a son had already been attended to by the firm. He was, however, granted access to his father's office. He searched through all the drawers of the desk and the files in the cabinet, putting aside a number of documents that seemed to be of interest. Yet he could not find what he was looking for. Not even in the cabinet, the key to which he found in the desk. The most important document, the contract containing the details of his father's pension, was nowhere to be found.

'My father's pension,' he asked the son-in-law, 'what exactly is the deal with that? I can't find anything about it, do you have the contract?'

'I don't think there was a contract. There was some arrangement between your father and my father-in-law, but nothing was ever put on paper.'

'I know for sure, my father told me about it.' Kamal was getting suspicious. 'There has to be a contract.'

The smile that appeared on the son-in-law's face confirmed Kamal's suspicions. 'Whether there was a contract or not doesn't matter. I don't believe there is a contract and I know he was only entitled to a pension during his life.'

No more was said about it. Kamal was baffled. He did not have a single piece of evidence and this man had stated point-blank that he, as the heir, could not claim the money his father had been due. Sixty thousand Swiss francs. Later in life he would often be reminded of that huge sum. The firm's lawyer had been a good friend of his father's, but in his anger he had forgotten that. He never thought of contacting him. A stupid mistake. Later he was convinced the lawyer would have helped him. It was only afterwards that he realised what he should have done, as would often be the case in his life.

His father's landlady gave Kamal two suitcases containing his father's possessions. Clothing, medication and documents that were of no great importance to him. Only the envelope with a cheque for two thousand six hundred Swiss francs interested him. It was a welcome addition to the savings he had been left. However, the bank refused to cash the cheque, because he had no proof of identity.

His father was dead, the civil war in Lebanon was worse than ever, and returning was not an option. He was alone in Switzerland, had no friends or family there and no job. The only thing he owned was the permit he had received on arrival, which would expire in a matter of days. He reported to the police in the Vaud district and asked for his permit to be renewed. He was given a three-month extension, three months to decide what the right direction was. But that was just what he lacked, a sense of direction. He had three thousand five hundred francs saved up, that was all. Germany seemed a likely destination. He had learned German at school, thanks to his father. But that journey would only be possible if somebody vouched for him, and he had no one who could do so.

He thought about his father and what he had done to get him into the country. He travelled to Geneva and reported to UNHCR. His name was on file and one day later he was received by an employee in a smart office. Kamal explained that he had no passport, only refugee status in Lebanon, and that he was here because of his deceased father. He added that he only had a travel pass for Switzerland and a permit that would expire in a couple of months. The official seemed sincere, made some notes and arranged a second appointment. She promised she would do what she could. Soon, however, it became clear there was nothing she could do for him and that he would not be allowed to stay. His application was denied.

At that moment, Kamal made his crucial mistake. He should have checked out of the hotel and reported to the police again, but he did not. He was not familiar with the procedure for obtaining refugee status in Switzerland. He should have told the police who he was, that he had no more money, that he had nowhere to go and no country of origin. He had subsequently discovered that he would have had a reasonable chance of being allowed to stay while his asylum application was considered. Under Swiss law he could not be sent back to Lebanon, which was a war zone, and Damascus had only ever been a stop along the way. It was summer in Lausanne and Kamal Kojadin, thirty-two years old, with an expiring residence permit, stayed at the hotel he should have checked out of. His money and his options were running out.

1945, ZAGREB

On 10 April 1945 Kamal's father closed the door to their home for the last time. The eight-storey apartment building was called the 'Skyscraper'. It was the tallest apartment building in Zagreb, a building of status, reserved for the higher social classes. The Kojadin family lived on the top floor with a fantastic view of the city, its large cathedral and the surrounding wooded hills. This would not be the last time he closed a door on their home and all their possessions.

Earlier that week his father had locked up his office at the Šuflajevoj Uliči, where he had been the last to leave. He was head of department at the central intelligence agency of the independent state of Croatia, a vassal state of Hitler's Germany. There, Saïm Kojadin had been dutifully working to destroy as many files as possible before the Partisans, the Yugoslavian national liberation army, came to take the city. The organization he worked for was comparable to the notorious *Reichssicherheitshauptamt* (Reich main security office) of Nazi Germany, whose task it was to arrest enemies of the state: communists, social democrats, liberals, journalists, resistance fighters operating in occupied areas and deserters.

Later Kamal heard that his father had packed many important documents in lead-lined chests and ordered them to be thrown into the Sava river. Fourteen chests, Kamal was told, but it is not clear whether this was true, as the chests have never been found.

The apartment building slowly disappeared in the distance. His father was no longer a high-ranking employee of the Croatian fascist regime, but a war criminal. He carried two suitcases and a bag containing important possessions. His mother, Sadeta Adinovic, held a travel bag containing gold and valuable jewellery and in her arms she carried their only child, Kamal, who was five months old. They were heading for Glavni Kolodvor, Zagreb's central station.

Kamal's father was from Travnik, an old provincial town now located in the heart of Bosnia-Herzegovina. Back then, however, it was still part of the Austro-Hungarian Empire. He was born in 1910 and, as the younger child in a Catholic family, trained to be a priest at the seminary in Travnik. He developed a serious kidney infection there, and was sent to a hospital in Munich for prolonged medical treatment. He stood out for his intelligence and eagerness to learn. A priest from Travnik sent a request to a fellow priest at a Munich monastery asking him to visit the patient. The priest felt sympathetic towards the talented young man who quickly learned to speak German, and he offered him the possibility of continuing his training in Germany. And so the twenty-four-year old was able to finish his training at a monastery in Munich at a time when the Roman Catholic Church was supporting the rise of Adolf Hitler. That had an influence on him. Kamal's father lived in Munich for five years. There he got to know Ante Pavelić, a political refugee from Yugoslavia, who had founded the fascist Ustaše movement.

Later he would become the leader of the Independent State of Croatia, the Nezavisna Država Hrvatska (NDH).

The Second World War was in its final, decisive phase. The US Fifteenth Airborne Division had taken off from Bari, Italy on 6 April 1945 to bomb Zagreb. Most of the bombs hit the airport. The beautiful, neoclassical railway station with its Corinthian columns remained unharmed and Kamal's parents managed to get hold of tickets for the train to Italy. Other members of the fascist regime had already done the same. The Catholic Church was prepared to protect them as refugees. Kamal's father knew what he had to do. Flee to Italy and get his family to safety.

For several years Ante Pavelić, born in 1889 in Bradina, southwest of Sarajevo, had been a member of the parliament of the Kingdom of Slovenes, Croats and Serbs that had come into being after the First World War. The new democracy did not function well and after a string of political crises, King Alexander seized power in 1929. He ruled the country as a dictator and Pavelić fled abroad. Five years later he plotted with his Ustaše movement to assassinate the king. The plot was successful, and the king met his end in Marseille.

The Germans marched into Zagreb on 10 April 1941. Cheering crowds welcomed them with flowers. The Independent State of Croatia was founded and Pavelić soon became its leader. He surrounded himself with a group of cronies with sympathies for Nazi Germany and fascist Italy, where he had lived in the years following the attack. The brilliant young Saïm Kojadin, whom he had met at the monastery in Germany, was among them.

Kamal's father was not like the most of the others, who were chiefly concerned about their own families, their own villages and their important contacts. He felt that those people, who were ostensibly serving the common good, were also in it for themselves, for their own honour and glory. Saïm Kojadin, on the other hand, was a man of deep faith and an even deeper belief in the ideal of a Greater Croatia, a territory that would encompass a considerable proportion of the Balkans and would define the face of Southeast Europe. It was this that united him and his comrades in the NDH regime.

Kamal's parents had found a space in one of the carriages. This train was one of many that travelled to Austria packed with refugees. There were passengers who feared Tito's advancing Partisan army, while others mostly wanted to secure their money. There were also soldiers in civilian clothes who had fought alongside the Germans. They would rather surrender to the British troops in Austria, where they expected to be protected and tried according to the laws of war, than fall into the hands of the communists and be transported to a prisoner-of-war camp. And then there were the high-ranking members of the Croatian regime and civilians with important positions in the NDH, such as Kamal's father, who were afraid to be captured by the Yugoslav People's Army and executed for collaborating with the Germans.

After Maribor the train meandered along the banks of the Drava towards the Austrian border. It stopped at several small stations where hardly anyone got off. The passengers had one common goal, to reach the border. Nearer the border the presence of the Allied Forces was more noticeable. At one of the stops, a few British soldiers boarded the train just as Kamal's father left the compartment to have a smoke. Not much later he returned to his wife.

'Keep calm and listen carefully,' he whispered. 'We have to get off, they're sending the train back.'

The soldiers had talked freely, probably assuming nobody could understand what they were saying, including the Croat who stood blowing smoke out of the half-open window. Kamal's father realised how sensible it had been to shave off his Hitler-inspired moustache. One of the soldiers was not aware of what was going on. The others explained to him that the British troops on the Austrian side of the border were not keen on receiving the steady stream of refugees who had started to flow in as the Partisans advanced. A deal had been made to send back everyone who arrived at the border. Saïm's English was excellent. He had understood them perfectly and immediately realised the danger they were in. His parents moved into the corridor, Kamal in his mother's arms. They did not know how close to the border they were and decided to leave the train as quickly as they could. The next stop was Prevalje, a station less than ten kilometres from the border. Two more passengers prepared to get off. That was fortunate, Kamal's father told him years later, as it meant they did not attract as much attention. They let the other passengers disembark first before getting off themselves. They left their suitcases behind in order to make it look like they were not refugees, but regular travellers returning to their village from Maribor. A man and a woman carrying a baby, both with only one bag, walked off the platform, expecting that somebody would call them back, that somebody would tell them they had forgotten their suitcases, but nothing happened. The train door closed.

Later it would be called a forgotten crime: the Bleiburg massacre. Kamal and his parents had managed to escape the terrible fate that had awaited them at the border. The passengers on this train and many others that reached the Austrian border during the final weeks of the war were sent back by the British soldiers, along with other refugees. They expected to reach a safe haven but ended up in the hands of Tito's troops. They were slaughtered en masse by the Partisans and dumped in mass graves.

~

Their journey continued along the densely populated roads in the border area between western Slovenia and Italy. They were engulfed by the stream of refugees that moved -either on foot or with the aid of carts, donkeys and cars -among troops who no longer appeared to have any control. Sometimes they walked twenty to thirty kilometres a day, Kamal's mother and father taking turns to carry him. Sometimes they would get a ride. His parents profited like many others from the general confusion in the final days of the war, and moving with this tide of human suffering, looking for safety, the family managed to reach Italy.

1945 - 1948, ROME

Kamal's father knew where to go in Rome and that he would be welcome even though he had arrived unannounced. The Eternal City was bustling with people in the final days of the war. Romans, raucous soldiers, refugees from many countries and the visitors who were constantly coming and going filled the city that Kamal and his parents crossed on their way to a monastery somewhere in the centre. Their destination was San Girolamo dei Croati, a church with a school and a guesthouse. A place of prayer, study and devotion to God. A place of hiding, too, a comforting sanctuary for refugees from the Balkans. But it was not the innocent victims of war who sought refuge in this place, for more often than not they were unable to. It was the guilty who were seeking shelter, and influential priests offered to keep them hidden. Krunoslav Draganovic was one of those priests, secretary of the brotherhood that ran the monastery of San Girolamo. He was an old acquaintance of Kamal's father. Krunoslav Draganovic and Saïm Kojadin had much in common. They had both been born and raised in Travnik, in the heart of Bosnia, spoke several languages fluently, were deeply religious, and put their home country, the independent Greater Croatia they so fervently wished for, before their faith.

Kamal and his parents crossed the Tiber and, walking across Ponte Cavour, reached Via Tomacelli. From there they could see San Girolamo monastery.

～

He was addressed as Dottore. Though Draganovic had an academic title, he was mostly called 'doctor' out of respect. The meeting turned into a reunion. Dozens of old friends, united through their Ustaše history, met again in San Girolamo, under the watchful eye of Krunoslav Draganovic, who took up their cause. In their eyes, they were all devout Catholics who had wanted to establish a 'Kingdom of God' in Croatia. Among them were acquaintances of Kamal's father, members of the NDH government and high-ranking officers, commanders of the Ustaše army. They included Ante Pavelić, the great leader of the NDH, who had fled to Italy through Austria, travelling from monastery to monastery. He was a remarkably cruel man and the most wanted war criminal in the Balkans. The Jasenovac concentration camp, a hundred kilometres from Zagreb, had been established on his command. The horrors that had been perpetrated there were on a par with those in the German camps. While the Germans had turned their camps into efficient genocide machines, the Ustaše camps were characterised by primitive cruelty and extreme sadism. Prisoners – children, the infirm and the old among them – were beaten to death with hammers, iron bars and hooks. People would be kicked to death, beaten with belts or leather whips on a daily basis. The Croatian camp guards would systematically hang, brand, freeze, choke, starve and gas prisoners. In 1942 about twenty-four thousand children were living within Jasenovac's barbed wire fences. Half of them were killed in cold blood and the other half died of starvation and neglect.

In San Girolamo, little Kamal was cradled by father Benares, the name Ante Pavelić used at the monastery. Kamal lay there in the arms of a child-murderer, a war criminal whose crimes equalled those of Adolf Hitler.

~

They were called 'ratlines', the escape routes used by the Nazis seeking a safe haven after the war. The routes mainly took them across Switzerland and Italy, the Catholic Church helping the war criminals to escape. It was not only the Croatian fascists who used these routes. The largest flow came from Germany, where almost the entire upper ranks of the SS were going up in smoke. When it became clear that Germany was going to lose the war, the SS officers turned their attention to preparing their escape. They provided themselves with false papers, dressed as civilians and abandoned their posts. They disappeared amid the chaos and benefitted from the mass migration that had begun in every direction during the final months of the war. The monasteries of the Catholic Church were staging posts on the way to Rome, which became a stepping stone to the Americas and the Middle East.

Doctor Draganovic, who had been so hospitable to Kamal and his parents, was at the hub of a ratline that offered new identities and a new life to Croatian war criminals. The monastery of San Girolamo ran a successful business creating new identities; false names were made up, papers were forged, travel documents from the Red Cross - acquired by the church - were exploited by war criminals, and new blank passports provided by the authorities of Brazil and Argentina were signed.

~

Although Kamal's parents had had to leave their suitcases on the train, they did manage to take their money, jewellery and gold with them in their hand luggage. After a few months in the monastery they rented an apartment in Rome. It was expensive, but they had the means to pay for it. Soon they managed to make a little money selling cigarettes. They became skilled at rolling the cigarettes, which they wrapped in fake Pall Mall packaging. They ran their small illegal business together with the Dervisevic family, whom they had met in Rome. Elez Dervisevic was also from Bosnia, and he and Saïm shared a vision of a Greater Croatia. This was the second war Elez had experienced. He had been born in 1901 and had joined the Austro-Hungarian army during the First World War. At just twelve years old he had fought in the famous Battles of the Isonzo. The army's youngest soldier, he was awarded a silver medal for bravery, along with five thousand forints. He had used this money to start a successful agricultural business. A wealthy man and a supporter of the Ustaše movement, he had fled Yugoslavia as the Partisans approached at the end of the Second World War. A long-lasting friendship developed between Kamal's father, the intellectual who had played an important role from behind a desk during the war, and Elez, the well-built soldier who had shown his mettle at the front. Little Kamal played with Ali and Ahmed, Elez Dervisevic's young sons.

Whether it was because of the cigarettes or because he was not able to present valid papers, no one remembers. The fact is that Kamal's father was arrested by British soldiers and transported to a prison just outside Rome. After ten days Kamal and his mother visited the prison on Via Tuscolana, on the way to Frascati. She noticed many children playing in the large courtyard. Kamal's parents decided that little Kamal should stay with his father. Several prisoners had brought a child with them and it seemed like a good idea to blend in. They also hoped it would prevent the British from treating him badly and digging into his past.

Kamal was three years old and he was in prison without realising it. Like the other children he played cowboys and Indians and hide-and-seek in the large courtyard. At first, his father thought Kamal's presence would be an advantage to him, but it was above all an inconvenience. Something was wrong with Kamal's foot and he was unable to walk. His father soon suspected something was amiss. The boy had not had his vaccinations and his father suspected it was poliomyelitis. They took him to the prison infirmary, where this diagnosis was soon confirmed. They started his treatment immediately, and the boy recovered. Not long afterwards Kamal caused another problem. He had long hair. His mother loved it, she thought he looked just like Joan of Arc. At playtime, one of the prisoners had been watching him and approached him. He offered him some sweets and asked him to come with him so he could make him look nice. Kamal did not resist. The prisoner took him to the barber's and had his hair cut. Kamal's girlish appearance had been bothering him. 'Now you look like a proper boy,' he said when the barber had finished.

When Kamal returned to his father he was furious. 'Who is the man who took you to the barber's? Point him out to me!'

Saïm knocked the man to the ground and stood over him. 'You have no idea why my son has long hair and what that means to me. He is my son, don't you dare interfere.'

Still furious, he turned to Kamal. 'And you. Now you see what happens when you go off with someone you don't know! Never, Kamal, never do this again!' These words stuck with Kamal for the rest of his life.

Until then Kamal's father had managed to remain inconspicuous, but the incident brought him unwanted attention. Sadeta, Kamal's mother, acted quickly, contacting a man from the Italian police who, at a price, could help Kamal's father. He knew a way to smuggle Saïm out of prison. On a visit to the prison, Kamal's mother had brought a map and instructions. The map would help him find his way from the prison to a house not far away. An Italian guard opened a door for them one night and Kamal and his father escaped.

~

Kamal and his parents lived at an address unknown to the British. The monastery of San Girolamo remained a meeting place. One of the buildings served as a refectory where refugees could go for a meal. Among the people who ate at the refectory was Malik Kulenovic. He was a mufti, an Islamic scholar who interprets and expounds Islamic law. He had fled the communists because of his faith. Kamal's mother was there to see Draganovic, who had arranged papers that would enable the Kojadin family to flee to Argentina. She saw the mufti washing dishes, and asked him why. Kulenovic was embarrassed as he replied that he was staying at the monastery and thought he should do something in return. Kamal's mother, who revered the mufti because of her Islamic background, grew angry.

'Stop that, you know who you are. You shouldn't be doing this kind of work.' She reproachfully turned to Draganovic.

'You know who he is, how could you let him do this?'

It had been a long time since Draganovic had been spoken to in this manner. He answered that Kulenovic should be grateful for being fed. Kamal's mother yelled at him that the faculty led by the mufti was worth ten times more than whatever Draganovic had ever done. The Dottore was deeply insulted.

'You are ungrateful, even though I have arranged the papers for you, your husband and your child.'

'Where are these papers?' Kamal's mother cried.

When Draganovic produced the papers from his inside pocket, she grabbed them from his hands and tore them up.

'I don't need your papers,' she yelled.

∼

'God made a mistake,' Kamal once said, 'my mother should have been born a man.'

Sadeta was a strong, proud, courageous woman. She was also strict and raised Kamal to be obedient. By tearing up the papers, Kamal's mother changed both the destination and the destiny of her family. She had read in the Italian papers that King Farouk of Egypt had announced he would allow three thousand families into his country. Muslim families that had fled the violence of war. He had even sent his private yacht 'Al Mahroussa' to Naples in 1947 to pick up the refugees. This was the same royal ship that the deposed Farouk would sail to Italy in after being overthrown in a coup in 1952.

Sadeta remembered the article and went to the Egyptian embassy. There was a war going on in Palestine and refugees could count on compassion from the Egyptians. Kamal's mother knew how to touch people's hearts, and she managed to secure permission for the family to travel to Egypt. A few weeks later Kamal and his parents left Rome with a visa for Egypt. The embassy paid for their passage on a boat called 'Pace', which means peace. The voyage took seven days via Istanbul and Alexandria. They arrived at the ancient harbour, where their new lives awaited them. There was a problem at border control, however. The embassy had made a mistake when it issued the visa. The numbers in the date of issue had been reversed and it now said 1984. The mistake was quite obvious and clearly the fault of a dyslexic clerk, but it was enough to send them back. They were not allowed to leave the boat, and were to return to Italy, get the papers renewed and come back.

'But that's impossible,' said Kamal's mother. 'The British are looking for us and we'll be arrested as soon as we get back to Italy.'

The captain was sympathetic and contacted the Egyptian consulate. 'There will be a diplomatic car waiting for you and it will take you to the consulate.'

They had three weeks to sort things out. A large black car with diplomatic plates was waiting for them at the harbour. The driver took them to the consulate, a splendid villa which would become King Farouk's home after his exile from Egypt.

Kamal slept next to his mother. On the first morning, there was a knock at the door. Sadeta asked who it was and a voice replied that he had brought them breakfast. The door opened and little Kamal was startled. He looked up at the man and was scared. This was the first time in his life he had seen a black man. He still remembers the name of the servant, Nur, a tall African man dressed in white Sudanese garments. Kamal and Nur soon got to know each other. The man showed him a playroom the likes of which he had never seen before. It was spacious, with a high ceiling, and it was filled with toys. The large rocking horse was what impressed Kamal the most. He spent fifteen days in paradise. Then he and his parents embarked once more on the voyage to Alexandria, this time with their paperwork in order. Yet again the importance of correct documents became very clear to them, because when they arrived, they were assisted by the Red Crescent, a humanitarian organization. When asked where they came from, they said they were from Yugoslavia. An interpreter who worked for the organization was called in. He told Kamal's parents they would remain in Alexandria for a couple of days before being taken to Cairo. There they would get what they needed to make a new life for themselves. The reception was quite cordial and no further questions were asked.

1948 – 1955, CAIRO

C oncrete and wood: these were the two parts to the former British Quar al Nil barracks in Cairo, located on the eastern bank of the Nile, close to the Egyptian Museum of Antiquities. The concrete buildings were reserved for high-ranking officers, the wooden barracks for the lower ranks. Like many other refugees, Kamal and his parents were assigned to the now empty wooden buildings. Officers of the Egyptian army were accommodated in the concrete part of the complex, strategically located in the heart of the city. Two different worlds, side by side on the eve of a coup, with one important thing in common: everybody was thinking about their future and weighing up their chances.

～

'You are a beautiful woman, but there are better ways of showing it.' Kamal's mother was talking to one of the Egyptian officer's wives.

'What exactly do you mean?'

'I mean you are a little overweight and with the right clothes you could conceal that.'

She had a gift for striking the right tone and made good use of her broken Arabic. Thanks to her clumsy choice of words and kind tone, the woman was open to her suggestions. Sadeta had a talent for making clothes and was looking for an opportunity to make a living. She could see that many of the officers' wives did not have a great sense of style and she planned to open a small sewing workshop.

'What do you think I should be wearing?' the woman asked. Sadeta offered to make her a dress. The woman accepted and asked her what she would need. 'I want to look for some fabric with you and I will need a sewing machine.'

They went into town and selected three different kinds of fabric. The officer's wife arranged for her to use a sewing machine. Kamal's mother took her measurements and told her to come back in a few days to try the dress on. She immediately set about measuring, cutting and threading. After a few days the dress was ready to be tried on. The officer's wife came over, put on the dress and looked in the mirror.

'This is beautiful, it's exactly what I wanted,' she said. Sadeta made some minor adjustments and finished the dress. The second dress was an even bigger success and the woman was absolutely delighted with the third. She offered to pay for it.

'We are friends, so one should not ask for money,' Kamal's mother said.

She was hoping to make dresses for more of the women and it seemed best not to ask for money at that point. The officer's wife was surprised. She was aware of the dressmaker's situation, that she was a refugee and depended on humanitarian aid.

'In that case I'll give you a small gift, a token of my gratitude.'

She put ten pounds in an envelope. In those days one pound was an ordinary worker's monthly salary in Egypt. She gave Sadeta the envelope and said, 'Don't open it now, do it when you get home and show your husband,' reasoning that Kamal's mother would not know what the money was worth and that her husband would inform her of its value.

Sadeta's tactics worked. The officer's wife told her friends that she wanted to introduce them to someone who knew what it meant to be a woman. After a week a group of officer's wives came over to make her acquaintance. Kamal's mother was a beautiful woman herself. She had greenish-blue eyes, light skin and long dark hair. She used barely any make up and did not need it. Her mere appearance, her gestures and her charmingly broken Arabic allowed her to establish a rapport with the women, who asked her to make dresses for them, too. They had brought fabrics with them and she inspected them. She told one of them, 'This fabric is beautiful and good quality, but the colour won't suit you. It would look better on her,' pointing to another woman. 'This one would look very becoming on you, we should switch them.'

She took their measurements and said she was afraid that she did not have a good sewing machine. One of the women said, 'I have a good machine at home. I'll send my driver over with it and you can give it back when you're done.'

And so Kamal's mother received a constant stream of orders and got paid for them. Slowly she achieved what she had set out to achieve: she came to be regarded as a friend, part of a group of prominent women.

◇

'Kamal sat on a princess's lap today,' his mother told his father one evening.

A delegation of the Red Crescent had visited the refugees at the barracks. A well-dressed older woman had talked to Kamal's mother while she was working in her little workshop. His mother explained that she made a little money sewing and the woman admired her for it. She asked if she could do anything to help. Sadeta did not hesitate to tell her that she was working with a borrowed machine and she could really use a more modern machine of her own. The woman proposed that they go and buy one immediately. Kamal held his mother's hand as they followed the woman. Outside the barracks a large black car stood waiting for them. A driver opened the door. The woman introduced herself as Princess Emine Tugay. She was immediately taken with Kamal and his girlish pageboy haircut, and not long after he was sitting on her lap as the splendid convertible made its way through Cairo, heading for the Singer shop. There, Kamal's mother was allowed to choose a new sewing machine, a gift from the Red Crescent. Later, his mother heard from one of her friends that the princess was a cousin of King Farouk of Egypt. Kamal once saw a portrait of the princess.

'She is the one I want to marry,' he declared.

Every few days Kamal's father went to a small newsagent's to buy cigarettes and magazines. Saïm did not speak Arabic, but after a few days he was able to ask the man what he owed him and a few weeks later the two were already having whole conversations. Kamal's father had acquired a French-Arabic dictionary – no Serbo-Croat dictionary was available – and he was quickly learning the language. At the newsagent's, Kamal's father asked a man if he knew of any jobs. The man asked him if he wanted to find work as a labourer or something else. Saïm said he was better equipped for an administrative position. He struck lucky. The man negotiated on his behalf at a wholesaler's, an import and export firm that traded in all sorts of commodities. Soon he was taking care of all the firm's correspondence with factories and business partners in several countries. It was an international role, perfect for someone with his talent for languages. It also paid well, earning him three Egyptian pounds a month.

~

Kamal was playing in the large courtyard between the barracks. He was being bullied and was defending himself by calling the bully names. The word he yelled was one he had heard the older boys use. He did not know what it meant, but he had seen the effect it had on others. Kamal's mother was just hanging her washing out. She did not quite catch what Kamal was yelling because he was swearing in Arabic. She wanted to know what it meant and so she made a mental note of the word. During coffee with the officers' wives, Sadeta mentioned the incident. She asked Lola, whom she was close to, what the word meant. Everybody heard what Kamal's mother said and started to laugh. She had not pronounced it correctly and they thought the way she said it was amusing.

'Say it again! What exactly did he say?'

They asked her to repeat the word three or four times. Everyone was laughing and Kamal's mother felt embarrassed. Lola and Sadeta went into the kitchen where she learned the meaning of the word. She was already angry for being laughed at and now she was even angrier. When she got home she did not say anything to Kamal, but waited for his father to return.

'Your son is going to turn out bad.'

Kamal's father was taken aback.

'Why? What makes you say that? I know my son.'

Sadeta told him what she had heard that day when Kamal was playing outside. His father did not take it too seriously. Yet his mother insisted that little Kamal would end up badly if he went on like this, that the barracks were not a good place for him and that he was being influenced by the wrong sort of friends. Sadeta's strict tone made Kamal's father give in and he told her he had a solution. Kamal was not told anything, but three days later he saw his mother packing his clothes in a suitcase.

'What are you doing, mum?'

'You are going on a trip with your father.'

'Where are we going?'

'Stop asking questions Kamal, you'll see.'

Saïm came home and asked Kamal to join him on a little walk, and he picked up the suitcase. When they arrived at an old building on the other side of Cairo, the big wooden door opened and a nun greeted them in Italian. Kamal's father asked to see the mother superior, with whom he also conversed in Italian. Kamal was listening and soon realised his father planned to leave him there. He had decided Kamal was to be educated by the nuns.

'But dad, why do I have to stay here?'

His father did not answer him. Kamal was seven years old and he was being separated from his parents. He did not understand and it felt like he was being punished. His father left. Kamal was angry and cried.

A month passed before his father came to see him again.

'Do you know why you're here, Kamal?'

He did not, and the nuns had not told him either. He was surprised to hear it was because of what he had said to the boy who had bullied him.

'It's a terrible insult to the boy's mother', his father claimed. 'Your mother sometimes gets so cross she hits you. I won't do that. I am doing this my way. You have to stay here and do your best. And now we are going to buy chocolate and fruit.'

For two years Kamal stayed at the school, educated by the nuns. It was a lesson in survival among children he did not know in an environment that was unfamiliar to him. During that time he learned to write Italian and Arabic. He had already learned to speak these languages on the street, including the Arabic word for motherfucker.

One of the first women Kamal's mother got to know was the wife of Habdel Fattah Gabri, an officer in the Egyptian army. She had made clothes for her and had told her about her life. The officer had heard they spoke Italian and he wanted to learn the language so he visited Kamal's parents. Kamal's father agreed to teach him and every week the man came down from his residence to the wooden barracks where the Kojadin family lived. After about a year Habdel Gabri had mastered the language quite well. He held an important position as a future general and this meant he sometimes had to go abroad for a few days. One day when he returned home from a trip, he found his wife in bed with another man. He did not understand. He was handsome, his position and prospects were good and they had three children together. He took out his gun and looked at his wife and her lover.

'What do you want me to do, kill you? I won't do that. But you, get out! And you, gather your belongings! We are going to get a divorce and the children will stay with me.'

And so it happened. Kamal's parents remained friends with the officer and he continued to come over for Italian lessons. Three months after Habdel's divorce, Sadeta asked him, as a friend, 'What are you going to do about your sons, your three boys? How are you planning to raise them properly? You need a wife.'

He listened to her.

'It's hard. I don't know if I can find a woman who'll do it, who can take care of my children.'

He stopped talking and seemed to be having trouble finding the right words.

'I need a wife, but not one who wants another child. I need an older woman.'

Kamal's mother said she knew a woman who would be right for him. He was curious and asked her who she had in mind.

'I can't tell you yet, I'm still working on it. I'll tell you soon.'

Fatah, victory, was the code word. The officers who were planning a coup used it during their secret meetings, some of which took place at the barracks, in Kamal's parents' house. The wooden barracks where the dressmaker to the officers' wives lived was a safe place. They were foreigners, they were friendly with some of the officers and had no interest in the matter. Gamal Abdel Nasser came over, along with other important figures in the coup of 1952. A general called Mohammed Naguib also attended the secret meetings of the Free Officers Movement. This general was considerably older than the young officers and the others held him in high regard because of his role during the Arab-Israeli War of 1948. Kamal's mother sometimes had coffee with the general's wife and once, when she was in the Naguib family's drawing room, she met Mohammed and said to him, 'I dreamt that something good is going to happen in Egypt. You will be president of this country.'

Mohammed Naguib tilted his head.

'What makes you think that?' He was surprised and slightly

suspicious. 'If that is God's will, that is what I shall be, but I doubt it, because I am a general serving under a king.'

'According to my dream, in less than ten days you will be president and the king will be forced to leave.'

Kamal's mother went home and stretched a canvas half the size of a door over a wooden frame and started to paint. She painted Naguib's portrait from a photograph. Kamal was watching. He had no idea his mother could do this. He was astonished – it was as if the general were about to step out of the canvas. In four days she painted Naguib wearing a uniform and cap. Kamal's mother covered up the painting, took it to Naguib's wife and asked her to put it in the living room and show it to her husband. She signed it and said it was her gift to him. Two days later Naguib came home and asked who had painted the picture.

'Our neighbour,' his wife replied.

He thought it was splendid. Kamal's mother knew how to impress people.

∼

Mohammed Naguib's younger sister thought of herself as an old spinster. She was about forty years of age and still unmarried. But Kamal's mother changed all that. She told Naguib she knew of a good husband for his sister.

'Who do you have in mind?' Naguib asked her.

Sadeta assured him he knew the suitor and told him Gabri's name. At that time he held a post in Tora, in the south of Cairo, where he was responsible for a military base and a prison for criminals and political prisoners. He was an esteemed commanding officer. Naguib approved and agreed to meet the man. Kamal's mother called Gabri and told him his new wife was ready to see him, but that he had to meet her brother first to seek his permission to marry her. Gabri agreed and asked her who this brother was. He was startled to hear it was Mohammed Naguib.

'I can't do that, he's my commander,' said Gabri. 'He's my superior, I'm not in any position to ask him.'

Kamal's mother, resolute as always, told him to leave it to her. She arranged the meeting and soon everybody was in agreement. Shortly afterwards they were married.

The coup took place on 23 July 1952, the group of officers unleashing a revolution. Tanks rolled through the streets of Cairo, but there was no violence and the main players, Mohammed Naguib and Gamal Abdel Nasser, drove through the city in an open-top car. King Farouk of Egypt had been overthrown. That evening a message was broadcast on the radio: the king had been arrested and Mohammed Naguib was now president of Egypt. Just as the radio was broadcasting this message, Kamal's mother got a phone call. It was Naguib telling her that her dream had come true.

Kamal's father proofread newspapers before they were printed and crossed out the articles he deemed inappropriate. He did this job on the side, having been asked personally by Mohammed Naguib. Kamal's parents no longer lived in the barracks. His father had found new employment, taking care of all the correspondence for a firm that dealt in leather imports from Greece. The pay was better and the family moved into an apartment on the third floor of a building closer to the centre of the city. Naguib visited there within a year of the revolution. He had a problem: he did not know anyone around him he could trust with the job of censorship. Behind the scenes, a power struggle was taking place among the officers. He needed someone to censor newspapers, illustrations, post and radio broadcasts. Somebody who was smart and level-headed.

'How can I find someone suitable for the job?'

Kamal's father realised immediately that Naguib was asking him and, despite certain misgivings, he agreed.

'I'll do it, but I would ask you not to keep me there for very long, because I don't want to lose the job I have now. I shall set things up and train others to do the work. But not for too long, because it's a hard job.'

From then on, no newspaper was printed before Saïm had read it. Whether it was published in English, French, Arabic or Italian, he checked them all.

Gamal Abdel Nasser, the most influential of the Free Officers, had taken charge and he did not want to lose Kamal's father. Mohammed Naguib had been deposed within two years, after the cunning Nasser won their power struggle. Kamal's father now worked at the ministry as head of the censorship department of the Mukhabarat, the intelligence agency founded by Nasser.

Kamal's father went to Nasser. 'I don't want to carry on with this job. I can't do it anymore, I'm tired. I work twenty hours a day, travel another hour, get no more than three hours' sleep, and I have a family.'

President Nasser did not agree and asked him to leave his other job and stay until they had found a suitable replacement. Kamal's father agreed to stay and kept working.

It did not take long before he proved himself invaluable to Nasser's regime. Whilst checking the post he discovered certain letters that did not seem quite right. Something was going on. By now he had developed a sixth sense for detecting slight abnormalities in correspondence, but he could not quite put his finger on it. He sent the letters on to an investigative department of the secret service, which uncovered a case of espionage. An Israeli spy had infiltrated the Egyptian government and was leaking classified information. Of course the Israelis were set on finding out who had unmasked the spy.

～

The Arab states and Israel were engaged in an arms race and tensions were running high in the region. Egypt had passed a law that denied any ship doing business with Israel access to Egyptian ports. One day in 1953 a letter from Cairo to Alexandria caught Saïm's eye. He noted the names of the addressee and the sender. It was a letter from a seaman to his sister. He opened the letter, which was written in Serbo-Croat and he read it. It said the seaman's ship would be in the port of Alexandria for five days for repairs and that their next port of call would be Tel Aviv. The seaman invited his sister to come and see him soon before the ship set sail again. This meant that the ship's captain had been lying about his destination, because he had requested to enter the port on his way to Sudan to repair a defect. A check was carried out that the Egyptians said was routine protocol. What was this ship's destination and what was it carrying? They found twenty-five million pounds' worth of weapons and munitions, presumably from Yugoslavia, headed for Israel. The cargo was confiscated and the ship and its crew were banished from the country.

～

The discovery of the spy had already stirred things up. Now came the revelation of the arms shipment. The Israelis and infiltrators in Egyptian circles started to worry about this unknown man who did such good intelligence work. The Israelis were now even more eager to find the person employed by the secret service who had uncovered all this. A Cairo-based member of Mossad, the Israeli secret service, was ordered to find out what was going on. Men with a certain position and prestige have their weaknesses, usually young and blonde. Mossad recruited some beautiful women and put them in touch with Egyptian officers who held key positions at the Ministry of Foreign Affairs, with orders to find out who was responsible for the espionage. Soon one of the women managed to extract information out of one of the officers. A Mossad agent contacted Yugoslavia, learned of Saïm Kojadin's background and grew suspicious. Mossad found out who had thwarted their plans and a nasty game ensued. They cleverly allowed the rulers of Egypt to learn that Mossad knew the true identity of their head of intelligence, and made him look bad. This undermined Saïm's position and his past made him vulnerable. It did not take long before he came to be regarded as a weak link, and therefore became expendable.

Kamal was playing with the dog when it suddenly started growling. Somebody was approaching the door and shortly afterwards the doorbell rang. His father was surprised. He was not expecting visitors on New Year's Day. Two men spoke with his father. Kamal could not make out what they were saying. His father came back in with a straight face and said, 'They want to put me in prison. They want to talk to me at the Ministry of Foreign Affairs first, but I believe they want to lock me up.'

Kamal and his parents were taken to the ministry. He and his mother waited all day while his father was being questioned. At one o'clock in the morning an officer came to tell them that Kamal's father was to be transported to prison and told them to go home. Kamal was shocked. This was the first big shock of his life.

'But he works for those people, how can they put him in prison?'

'It's not right, Kamal, it must be a mistake,' his mother answered soothingly, but this did not reassure him. He did not understand how his father, whom he admired so much and who did good work could be imprisoned by the very people he worked for. He was angry and confused. His dream was to become a pilot or aircraft designer and that suddenly seemed impossible. His father had been his wings and, now that he had been arrested, Kamal's dream seemed to have flown away.

Kamal's mother sought help. Gabri, the general who had studied Italian with his father, was unable to help them. Sadeta sought out the other officers she knew well, but got the same response. It was out of their hands, one of the officers said. It was impossible for them to do anything. Kamal's mother grew more and more angry. She eventually managed to get hold of Nasser.

'My husband worked for your country, for your people. You have to let him go!'

She asked what he was being accused of and discovered Mossad's game. The Egyptian intelligence agency had been misled and was under the assumption that Saïm was just pretending to be a Muslim. They accused him of espionage and of taking a Muslim name though he was not a Muslim. Nasser also told her he could not help them. He did not want a conflict with the Minister of Foreign Affairs and he had other interests. He said, 'I know he has done good work for us, I know who you are, but I can't do anything.'

Kamal's mother knew how politics worked. Nasser, the most powerful man in Egypt, simply did not want to do anything. Thanks to the rumours the Israeli secret service had spread in Egyptian circles Kamal's father was now regarded as a spy.

∼

Kamal cried at night, but he made sure his mother did not know.

He knew she was suffering too but that she was keeping it from him. Kamal's father was kept under lock and key at the ministry and was later transported to Tora prison twenty kilometres outside Cairo. Kamal and his mother had the right to visit once a week. One day Kamal's mother said, 'We barely have anything to eat and no money, what are we to do?' Her tone was desperate. It was the first time his mother had shared her concerns with him and asked his advice. Kamal was ten years old and he suddenly felt a lot taller. Kamal's father had always kept his job with the leather import company and Kamal felt he should take on his father's role. He proposed that he go to the owner for money. It was the first time Kamal had gone into town by himself. He felt like a man, a man on a mission. Kamal went to the office of Cohen, the owner, and politely said, 'My father is in prison, and my mother and I need help. We have run out of money. Can you help us?'

Cohen looked at Kamal, opened a desk drawer, took out fifty Egyptian pounds and put them in an envelope.

'Tell your mother I'm sorry, I cannot help you, as it would be the end of me too.'

The money was not charity. Cohen understood only too well that Kamal's father's situation was serious and that he had no influence. He was scared and, given his Jewish background, wanted to avoid taking any risks.

'Tell your mother she mustn't send you here again, it isn't wise.'

~

Kamal filled a small bottle with liquor, the rakia his father had asked for. Every week he visited the prison with his mother. With the bottle in his waistband he would sit on his father's lap, and he would unobtrusively take it out and slip it into his own pocket. Kamal relished this exciting game and the joy it gave his father. It was the summer of 1955 and his father had been in prison for six months. His mother had been living off their savings, but there was not much left. Kamal's father decided something had to be done. He had to get out of prison and he realised they only stood a chance if they were willing to leave Egypt. Saïm thought it might be possible to go to Damascus. He had a few acquaintances from Croatia there that might be able to help them. Kamal's mother clung to this prospect. A short time later they found that the Egyptian government was willing to give them fourteen days to leave the country. After ten days an official from the ministry came to Sadeta's door with papers that would allow the family to travel to Damascus. The documents said they were refugees. The journey was financed by the government. They were allowed to take only what was absolutely necessary. Once more they left everything behind and headed for the airport, where they met up with Kamal's father and boarded the plane for Damascus. Kamal was crying. He kept thinking of the dog they had to leave behind.

1955-1958, DAMASCUS

His mother had been given a little note with a phone number on it. She had been told to call it as soon as they arrived in Damascus. The contact would help them on their way. He was a civil servant, an official from the Syrian Ministry of Foreign Affairs, who would arrange documents and accommodation for them.

The papers Kamal's parents received reaffirmed their status as refugees. There had been contact between Egypt and Syria, and the official was familiar with their situation and background. Kamal and his parents were assigned a one-bedroom apartment in a drab building that also housed other refugees. They received some basic clothing and furniture and a little money at the beginning of each month.

~

They called themselves the Domobran, the Croatian Home Guard. Kamal's father was a member and there were other members living in Damascus with whom he soon made contact. Domobran was a political and military organization established in 1928 that campaigned for an independent Croatia. The extreme right-wing network remained active even after the Second World War in countries where Ustaše members had sought exile.

Syria and other Arab countries had gladly welcomed a large number of Nazis, mainly because they were military experts. The knowledge of these war criminals was welcome in the Middle East and their past was not regarded as a problem. Old acquaintances of Kamal's parents from the time during and immediately after the war, such as Hasan Custovic, Elez Dervisevic and Ada Zubcevic, all former Ustaše members, joined the Syrian army as instructors in 1947 and fought alongside them in the war against Israel in 1948. Old friends, old comrades they were, who had sworn their loyalty to the same cause and who still had each other's backs, no matter what was going on.

∾

'I could make a champion out of you, I will talk to your father,' the pool superintendent said to Kamal. He was learning to swim at the pool not far from his house. Kamal was a fast learner who had remarkable strength, and remarkable toes. On each foot, two toes had grown together. His webbed feet made Kamal faster in the water. The superintendent had a beer with his father and Kamal listened as they discussed his feet.

'It is not a major operation,' the superintendent proclaimed, who thought that joining the other toes to the ones already grown together would make him invincible in the water. Kamal's father frowned at him.

'He is already big and strong and with feet like that he is sure to become a champion,' the superintendent attempted to persuade Kamal's father.

To Kamal's relief, it was clear his father did not agree. Kamal would like to be a champion, but not at the expense of his toes.

It took a while for Kamal to get used to school, as education in Syria was not the same as in Egypt. His father and the principal of the school discussed what class he should join. Because Kamal was larger than the other boys his age, the principal had decided to place him in a class two grades higher. During lessons, he often had trouble understanding the teachers and found the material difficult. Kamal felt lost and started to lag behind. His father saw that he was unhappy and arranged for a teacher to tutor him at home. It was a great relief that his father understood and managed to find a solution. Kamal looked up to his father; the quiet, often introverted man, who knew so much, who patiently dealt with his mother's vagaries, attentively inquired about his life and who showed him the appreciation he so badly needed.

～

One of the other Domobran members had helped Kamal's father get a job. That is what old friends are for, after all. He now worked as a translator at Radio Damascus, Syria's broadcasting station, but he was soon looking for another, better job. He responded to an advertisement in the paper placed by a lawyer who had a permit to trade with foreign countries. Faris Daw was looking for someone to take care of his international correspondence, mostly in French. Kamal's father got the job. Most of the business involved dealing in jewellery. Not real gems, but industrially produced imitations. Daw had set up a ring of traders who sold the jewellery in the streets. Syria was an up-and-coming country in the Arab world. The economy was growing; money was being made and spent. Dew's peddlers were turning a good profit.

Step by step, their new life started to take shape. Kamal was going to school again, his father was working and he kept in touch with his old friends. Only Kamal's mother had trouble adjusting. She was almost forty years old and her rheumatism was getting worse. She had difficulty walking and could no longer work. Her four Singer sewing machines had had to remain in Egypt. She had been successful there, with six women working for her. She would give them assignments, check the work and sit down in the evening, satisfied. Her life had changed. She thought back to that time and had trouble believing she had actually done those things. But now her body was failing her, which only made her more angry and defiant.

More than fifty years later, Kamal still remembers exactly how he felt when he got the clout on the ear. His father had never hit him before. This was the first time and it was not the pain of the blow but his father's rejection that stayed with him. He was fourteen years old and he already had a good idea of what was going on. Not because his parents ever discussed anything with him, but because he was clever. By piecing together what he heard them talk about, he started to construct his own story about his parents' lives. He found his father's past in Yugoslavia especially intriguing. The NDH and Pavelić, the boastful stories of his father's Ustaše friends. He also observed that his father never joined in with their boasting and kept his thoughts to himself during conversations of that kind. He wondered why. He did not remember what exactly he had asked, but when he probed his father about his work in the Balkans one day, he received that clout on the ear and the words, 'Remember one thing: forget the Balkans and never ask about it again!'

His mother had yelled that they had gone insane and that there was no justice to be had. Kamal understood his parents had been given notice that they had to leave the country, again. The Syrians feared a communist take-over and had looked to Egypt for help. The two countries had decided to merge into a single state, the United Arab Republic. From February 1958 onwards the Egyptians became very influential in Syria. A couple of months later they made it clear that Kamal's father could not stay there for the same reason he had been banished from Egypt. Once again, it was time for the Kojadin family to leave.

1958 -1976, BEIRUT

The air was fresh and full of aromas, so unlike Damascus. Kamal enjoyed the air, the fresh fruit, the spicy Lebanese food, the hospitality and his first bottle of 7Up.

The Syrians had given his parents permission to go to Lebanon. The family crossed the border in early June 1958. They had been given the name of a man who owned a small guesthouse in Stura, just across the border. Selim Kassouf, the landlord, turned out to be an amiable man the same age as Kamal's father. Saïm handed Selim a letter written by the Syrians. The man read the letter and tears welled up in his eyes. The letter was short, but those few words made it clear to Selim what Kamal and his parents had gone through. He welcomed them, reassured them and told them it would be wise to stay there until the revolt in Lebanon was over.

By mid-July, American marines had helped the Lebanese regime put a stop to the turmoil. Selim came to tell them it was now safe for them to leave for Beirut, almost a hundred kilometres away. Kamal's stay in Stura had lasted twenty-five days.

'I don't want to leave. Can't we stay here?' Kamal asked. To him it all felt like a long holiday.

~

Pension Anna, a guesthouse on Allenby Street, was named after the owner. The landlord in Stura had recommended it to Kamal's parents and had arranged for a taxi to take them from the border town to Beirut.

'Call me when you get there and let me know if all is well,' Selim had said.

Anna turned out to be an Armenian woman of about sixty-five, an immigrant. When she was young, like many of her fellow Armenians, she had fled from the communists after the Soviet Union invaded her country in 1920. She knew what it was like to be a refugee and Kamal's parents felt she understood them. Kamal wandered through the rooms of the guesthouse with their four-metre-high ceilings, which reminded him of the room with the toys at the Egyptian consulate in Rome.

The guesthouse was situated on the fifth storey of an old building. The windows afforded a magnificent view downhill towards the port. Kamal could see ships setting sail from there. Now and then, he would still hear the sounds of automatic weapons and of bombs exploding. They were the last-ditch efforts of the rebel Muslims. It was a short conflict that was soon resolved, and gradually peace was restored to the Lebanese capital.

~

Anna had contacts in the upper echelons of Beirut society. She knew a man with a large import and export business. The firm was called Najjar Continental and it was also located on Allenby Street, the wide road that led to the port. The owner was looking for someone to deal with the international correspondence. Saïm applied for the job, and the owner, Najjar, asked him to write a letter to a business contact in Germany. Kamal's father said, 'If you give me the last letter they sent you, then I will answer it. Tell me what you want from them.'

Najjar explained and Kamal's father sat down at the typewriter and typed the letter on the spot. He handed it over and said, 'If the letter is good, sign it.' Najjar read the letter and signed it. Kamal's father was hired.

The German firm soon replied. It was clear from the response that Saïm had written a flawless letter. The firm answered that they were happy that Najjar was now employing a German, which would improve their communication. Najjar knew that he had found a valuable asset in Saïm Kojadin. His first salary was three hundred Lebanese pounds, but Najjar was soon paying him double.

After five months, Kamal and his parents moved from Anna's place to a house of their own on Mohammad Al Hout in the centre of Beirut. His father was making enough money for them to live a normal life again, although Kamal did not quite realise it at the time. He still took life for granted, whether he was living in the barracks in Egypt, a small apartment in Damascus, a guesthouse in Stura or their new home in Beirut.

The Paris of the Middle East was what people called the Beirut of 1950 - 1975. It was a golden age for Lebanon. The country was politically neutral, the population was ethnically diverse and the mutual tolerance that existed there was unparalleled in the region. The atmosphere was open and liberal. Beirut was lively by day and vibrant by night. Kamal felt happy as he wandered through the shopping area and saw jeans in a shop window for the first time, even though he did not have the money to buy a pair. Jeans had been banned in Syria.

Kamal attended Lebanon College, where he had trouble keeping up. People spoke French at school and he was behind on the curriculum. He did not know the language, which made him fall behind even more and he had little contact with his classmates. He felt unhappy and alone. Mathematics was the most difficult obstacle. He could not grasp the connection between letters and numbers in algebra, and geometry was a complete mystery to him. He realised that his dream of becoming an aircraft designer or mechanic would never come true. His mother was not sympathetic and kept sending him to school, day in and day out. Under his breath, Kamal would refer to her as 'the boss'. She was often bad-tempered because of the increasing discomfort caused by her rheumatism. She was used to giving orders, to supervising and managing everything, and now she no longer could. She clung to her role, ruling the lives of her husband and son from their home. She was the one who did the talking; Kamal was merely supposed to listen. His mother never asked him about school or his plans. Not because she did not love him, but because she was always so occupied with herself that there was little space for anybody else. Kamal grew up in his mother's sizable shadow.

She truly loved movies and often ordered Kamal to accompany her to the cinema. She had trouble walking and needed support. But Kamal did not mind the weekly cinema visits. The sophisticated city of Beirut had a considerable number of cinemas and they would often visit the Roxy, the Imperial, Radio City, Al Hamra or the Rivoli. They would screen Hollywood movies and Kamal got to know the great stars of the screen. Clark Gable and Anthony Quinn were his mother's favourites while he was hopelessly in love with Doris Day.

∾

'You are going to boarding school,' Kamal's father said.

Kamal was still having trouble settling in at secondary school. His father regarded a good education as vital, it was something he had benefited from his entire life. One of the best schools in Lebanon was Collège Saint Joseph in Aintoura, situated in the hills of the Keserwan District north of Beirut. The school, run by Jesuits, had existed for centuries, and was attended by the children of the best families in Lebanon. By this time Kamal's father had already established enough contacts to secure a place for his son and Kamal knew that his father would brook no opposition in such matters. And so, by the autumn of 1960, he was headed for Aintoura. He only returned home one weekend a month. Again Kamal was living in a monastery, this one situated on a hill covered with pine trees. It was a large building of yellow stone surrounded by a beautiful garden, with arcades and walls covered with biblical murals. It was there that Kamal learned to speak several languages. The curriculum was structured in such a way that every few months he would get a new teacher who spoke a different language. At the beginning of the year, he was taught in Arabic, then three months in French and after that they were assigned an English teacher. He felt much more at home here. The gap between him and the other children was not as wide as it had been at his school in Beirut and it did not take long before he had found his place among his classmates. He socialised with the children of wealthy families, establishing friendships that would be of use to him later. Though he did not belong to this elite, he was accepted because of his charm and his classmates considered him one of them.

'Bouteille.'

'Bottle', answered Kamal.

'Chemin.'

'Road.'

His father's eyes were scanning the room.

'Panier.'

'Easy,' said Kamal, 'birdcage.'

Sometimes it felt like a competition when he was home in Beirut. His father would call out a word in one of the languages he had already learned and Kamal would tell him what it meant. Usually he knew the right answer and he would sense his father's approval. Now and then, his father would call out a German word he did not know. It annoyed him, not least because he knew he could not win this game against his father. One day, his father asked him if he wanted to learn German, too. Kamal was keen, hoping that one day he would win the language game.

~

Kamal had never been surprised by his father. He took it for granted that he had contacts everywhere, that there was always someone there to help them out. It was only later that he found out this network of old friends was always present, like an invisible safety net. So he did not ask questions when a friar at Aintoura came to see him to inform him that his father had found him a German teacher and that he would be able to start lessons soon.

It turned out that his teacher lived at the monastery too, and only later did Kamal start to suspect it was no coincidence his father had asked him if he wanted to learn German, that his father knew of this teacher. The French Jesuits at the monastery called him Frère André, but after a few lessons, Kamal found out that his name was actually Andreas. He had been born to German parents in Alsace-Lorraine, which had been part of the German empire until the end of the First World War, when it reverted to French rule. Andreas had been raised in this border area and had grown up bilingual. Kamal and Brother André communicated in French as they studied German grammar. In the beginning, his teacher was not very talkative, but as they progressed, he started to talk more openly to Kamal. One day, Kamal told him that he and his parents were from Croatia. The teacher did not seem surprised and said he understood how Croatians think.

'We had a strong alliance, Germany and Croatia,' he said. 'The Croatians and the Germans still love each other. But not the Serbs, they can't forget the war and still want revenge.'

Slowly, Kamal and his teacher started to confide in each other. They would talk about the things that Kamal was so keen to hear more about, the issues that were taboo with his father. Kamal talked to him about the war, about Nazi ideology and relations between countries. The teacher told him what he had done during the war, what had been expected of him and how, as a young man, he had not asked questions. Only later, as a refugee, had Andreas started to think about the repercussions of the things he had done. He told him he was wanted by the Americans and the British and that this was why he was living in Lebanon. The country was a safe haven for refugees, but not those who were suspected of war crimes. The teacher was also a wanted man, but he had managed to pass himself off as a friar and find asylum in Aintoura. Andreas told him he regretted his actions. He never answered Kamal's questions as to what these actions had been. Kamal never found out more than that Andreas had been a pilot with the Luftwaffe and, later, a member of the SS.

For almost two years, Kamal studied German and his teacher was like a father to him. Years after he left Aintoura, he found out his teacher had died of cirrhosis of the liver. Kamal was not surprised, recalling the many bottles of wine Andreas had asked him to buy at a shop near the monastery.

After several years in Aintoura, Kamal returned to Beirut to complete his education at a private school. He was nineteen years old when he graduated and started to look for work. He met an Italian who dealt in yarn who offered to employ him for a trial period as a middleman in the Beirut area. Kamal had grown into a young man of medium height, though he was taller than most Arabic men. He was not particularly handsome and he had a very prominent nose. His appeal lay in his charming smile and in his gestures. Often, during a conversation, he would place his hand on the arm of whomever he was talking to and call him by name, creating an intimacy that left an impression. Because of his talent for sales, he was allowed to stay on after his trial period, and worked for the Italian for almost two years. He was earning his own money for the first time, lived with his parents and enjoyed spending his money in his free time in the vibrant city of Beirut. Kamal was on his way to becoming an adult, and was discovering the city's nightlife. In 1964, Louis Armstrong had overtaken the Beatles in the American top 100 with his song 'Hello Dolly'. In the years that followed, he toured Africa, Europe and Asia. Kamal was in the front row when Armstrong performed in Beirut.

In time, he found he wanted to do more than sell yarn. He applied for classes at evening school in some subjects he needed to get into the Economics Faculty at the university. He signed up for the course, but soon decided to quit. He realised he had had enough of book learning. He was still keen to learn, just not in that way.

At evening school, he had become acquainted with a boy whose father owned a jewellery workshop. Kamal was interested in this practical trade, as he liked working with his hands. He asked the boy to introduce him to his father so he could apply to be an apprentice. The boy passed on the request to his goldsmith father, who discovered that the boy and his parents did not live far away. One evening, when the boys were at school, he visited Kamal's parents. He explained that he could do with an apprentice, but since he worked with such valuable materials he would not take on just anyone. He wanted to be convinced his new apprentice had a good background, so he spoke to Kamal's father. He soon became convinced that he was trustworthy and decided to hire Kamal. After their conversation, Kamal's father asked, 'What do you want me to do?' The goldsmith answered, 'Nothing. Your son does not need to know we had this conversation. I will tell my son that Kamal can come to my workshop and I will hire him. But I won't pay him for the first year, just train him'.

For the first year, Kamal did nothing but clean. The tables, the machines and the floor had to be cleaned meticulously. All the sweepings had to go into the kiln because of the miniscule particles of precious metals that were swept up with the dust. Kamal complained sometimes, but the owner was resolute and frequently explained that every apprentice must start at the bottom. Nevertheless, he learned a lot about the trade, because he was intrigued by the things he saw. The melting and pouring of the metals, the hammering and embossing, the moulding and setting. He paid attention to how the others worked, committed lots of things to memory and came to realise that, while knowledge was important, applying it was a real skill.

'Come, I want to show you something,' the owner said almost a year after Kamal had started working for him. He showed Kamal how to make settings for gemstones. Kamal felt that the real job had started. After five or six days he had mastered the technique and the owner was satisfied. Then the goldsmith gave him several copper rings, saying, 'I shall now teach you how to set in copper. Imagine the copper is gold and the bits of glass are diamonds.' He gave Kamal a few small stones made of glass, sat down next to him and demonstrated what needed to be done. He took a grinder and some other tools. Kamal looked on and said, 'Now let me try.'

He picked up the tools and positioned the stone. It was a delicate job. He did a few more and the owner was surprised. Though Kamal had large hands and thick fingers he handled the tools and small stones very dexterously. Then it was time to start fixing the stone. He picked up the appropriate tools.

'You have to apply a little more pressure there,' said the goldsmith when Kamal had difficulty. So he applied a little more force, but the glass broke.

'You're very strong. You need to work carefully and slowly increase the amount of pressure you apply.'

This was the most difficult task for Kamal, using the right amount of force to fix the stone after setting it. Little by little, he learned to do it properly. After six months, he was ready. It was time to start work with real gold and diamonds.

'Don't put too much pressure on it,' the smith said, 'but make sure the stone is firmly set and can't fall out.'

'Can the diamond break if I apply too much pressure?' Kamal asked. He was a little nervous now that he was handling real gold and diamonds.

'You have to get to know the stones. If a stone is likely to break under five kilos, you should apply about two-and-a-half kilos of pressure. It is an art, a feeling, but if you have the right feel for it, you are going to love this trade.'

And that is precisely what happened. Kamal steadily improved and became absorbed by the work. After three years, he had gained a lot of experience.

～

'We're done, and now that you have so many skills, I can no longer afford you,' his teacher said. 'You can get a better salary elsewhere and keep improving your skills. You should start looking for something else.'

Kamal understood and was also eager to take the next step. He asked the goldsmith for advice.

'Kamal, the money you have earned here in the last few years, have you spent it all?'

Kamal had actually lived quite frugally. He still lived with his parents and since he had started to work with the goldsmith he had pretty much stopped going out in the evening.

'No, I've got money,' he said.

'How much have you saved?'

Kamal told him he had three-and-a-half thousand dollars, a large sum at that time.

'Really?' The owner could not believe it. 'Well done, boy,' he said and opened a window. 'Come here and take a look.'

He pointed out a window on the opposite side, a little further down the street. 'Do you know who lives there?'

'Yes, I do, that is George's workshop.'

'Exactly. And George wants to sell his business and go to America. Go to him and tell him you want to buy his workshop. I know he will ask for too much money, but I believe the money you have saved will be sufficient. Try to do a deal with him.'

Nervously, Kamal entered George's workshop. He had been inside before, but this time he looked at the place with new eyes. It was smaller than the workshop he had trained in, but all the important machinery, tools, workbenches and tables were there. It was clean and the place seemed to be in good repair. George gave him a warm welcome and, while he looked around, Kamal kept the conversation going and soon began to feel the last of his doubts evaporating. He wanted to buy this business.

'I heard you want to sell the business and the workshop. That you want to go to America.'

George nodded and told Kamal about his plans. Casually, Kamal asked about the price.

'Five thousand dollars,' George said.

'I can't give you that, I don't have that much money.'

George was surprised, he had not expected this response. 'Oh, are you looking to buy my business?'

Kamal confirmed that he was. Now it was his turn to be surprised by George's response.

'You can have the business for two thousand dollars. I don't want any more. Take it or leave it.'

Kamal did not have to think for long and they closed the deal with a handshake. Still stunned that he had done the deal for two thousand when George had initially wanted five, he returned to the goldsmith.

'Did you buy it?'

Kamal told him he had put in a bid for two thousand dollars and that George had accepted it. He thought it would be a good idea to adapt the story a little now that he was a businessman.

'Did George accept that? It's a gift. You're lucky, Kamal. I hope you are successful and that you won't take my customers with you.'

'I won't do that. I think I'll have enough of a job keeping George's customers happy.'

It was 1968 when Kamal went into business. He had refugee status in Lebanon and he applied for a working visa, which was granted.

The Lebanese economy was booming, and Kamal profited from the country's growing prosperity. He was doing so well that he was able to hire an employee after six months. After a year he rented a small shop down the street where he could sell everything that was being produced in the workshop. Two years later, he was employing six people and spent most of his time managing and inspecting his business. At twenty-six years old, Kamal was running a successful business in Beirut.

〜

'I'm looking for an interpreter, someone who speaks both Yugoslavian and Arabic,' Boris Bosinov said. 'Someone who can help me start a business, although I'm not sure what kind of business yet.'

Lebanon was like a magnet to people in search of business opportunities. Boris was one of them. In spite of the vagueness of his plans, Kamal had faith in the man and had been fascinated by him from the moment they met. They had been introduced by a Bulgarian he did business with. He knew the Balkans well and Kamal enjoyed talking to him, not just about business, but also about the world his parents had come from. The Bulgarian had called and invited him to his office to meet one of his fellow countrymen. It was there that Kamal first shook hands with Boris Bosinov. 'He reminded me of a lion,' Kamal said later. He was surprised by the man who, despite being about sixty-five years old, was vigorous, strong and full of ambition. Boris was from the Ochrid region, in what is now Macedonia, which was governed by the Bulgarians at the time. He and Kamal spoke the same language. Since Boris did not know any Arabic, he was now looking for an interpreter. Their shared provenance created a special bond between them and now and then Kamal would accompany Boris when he needed an interpreter. Together, they enquired as to what kind of business opportunities there were for Boris, but met with little success at first.

'I am looking for someone who owns a suitable piece of land where I could start a flower business,' Boris said one day.

It wasn't a bad idea, Kamal thought. He knew a lot of people because of all the schools he had attended. For years his classmates had been children from wealthy families, so Kamal had contacts among the prosperous elite. As a student, he had had the advantage of being seen by his friends' parents as a foreigner and somehow independent. They trusted him and enjoyed showing him their country and their world. He often visited his friends at home and was always warmly received. Kamal was always careful to make a good impression. He was intelligent, well-spoken, multilingual and looked good. He had kept in touch with many of the contacts he had accumulated over the years.

'I know somebody who has bought a large piece of land for the expansion of Beirut airport. Let's go and see him.'

Kamal called and arranged a meeting. With Kamal's help, Boris explained his plan to the Lebanese landowner. He also made it clear that, although it was a good idea and he was enterprising enough to make it a success, he himself did not have the financial resources to invest in it. It soon became clear that the landowner was not very interested in someone who could not bring any money to the table. Kamal had feared this might be the case.

'The only thing that matters to many Lebanese is whether you have money. That is how they decide if they like you or not,' Kamal whispered to Boris in Yugoslavian. In the end, the landowner agreed to lease him the land, but only on condition that he receive fifty percent of the profits.

'I want to rent the land for twenty years for a good price, build a business and live off the profits. I am not going to give away half of my earnings to someone who just sits and looks on. Thanks a lot,

I'm sorry for disturbing you.' Boris abruptly cut short the meeting, leaving the Lebanese landowner bewildered.

Although Kamal saw that Boris had not accomplished anything with his forthright attitude and his crude language, he was still in awe of him and he decided to be more resolute himself. He was usually friendly and keen to avoid conflict. Though he often managed to get his own way, he would sometimes hide his annoyance, keeping himself in check when he would rather speak out.

~

When he had met Kamal, Boris Bosinov had asked him about his line of work but had not mentioned it since. Now he broached the subject again.

'Kamal, I know a thing or two about the business you are in. Do you think you could put me in touch with someone I could work for in this profession?'

Kamal thought Boris was implying that he would like to work for him and immediately told him he was already employing six people. Boris explained that that was not what he was after. He claimed he had other plans. Kamal showed him around in his workshop and found that Boris did indeed know a lot about the profession. He asked Kamal where he bought the settings for his gemstones. The silver, gold and platinum settings were bought in rather than being made by hand. Because of the way he asked, Kamal got the impression Boris had something in mind that he was not saying.

'Could you introduce me to the person who crafts these settings?'

Kamal introduced Boris to a man he knew well, who had machines that were especially suited for working gold. The machines were used to mould the gold, under pressure, into different elements like the gemstone settings. Not long after Kamal had introduced Boris to him, he heard that his Bulgarian friend had started working there. The owner told him that Boris was doing excellent work. Making settings involves a certain technique that uses a special hydraulic machine. Boris was familiar with the technique and had made some adjustments to the machine so the settings could be produced more quickly and efficiently. This had raised the rate of production and the owner was very pleased with his new employee.

Kamal received a call from Boris to ask if he had time to come and visit the workshop where he was working. He needed Kamal to be his interpreter for an important conversation, and he was hoping for his support, too.

'Could you ask him if he has a British gold pound?'

Kamal asked the owner of the workshop. He replied that he had, opened the safe and retrieved the valuable coin.

Boris took the coin and said, 'I can make these too.'

Kamal looked at him incredulously. 'How?'

'I'll show you. Ask the boss to give me the right amount of gold. I know the exact blend, this coin is not pure gold. It costs less to make this coin than it is worth.'

'Are you certain?'

'Indeed I am, Kamal. Let me demonstrate.'

Kamal translated what Boris had said.

'Give him enough gold for ten coins,' Kamal suggested. 'Then we will send them to a laboratory to be analysed.'

The owner agreed to give Boris the required amount of gold.

Boris set to work, first producing the moulds for both sides of the coin. He did not want anyone to see what he was doing, so he worked on the coins in secret during the evenings. When the moulds were finished, they needed to be placed in a press, a machine that applies pressure at either fifteen, thirty or forty tonnes. The owner had a thirty-tonne minting machine. Boris used the machine, putting three tonnes of extra weight on it without anyone seeing, in order to achieve the right result. He made ten coins and said, 'Go and get them tested. You'll see they are legitimate.'

The laboratory soon delivered the results. The etching was perfect and so was the composition of the material. Kamal had many contacts in the jewellery business and soon he and Boris used them to sell the coins. It was a profitable business. This is how, without fully realising it, Kamal ended up in the world of counterfeiting. In Medieval times, counterfeiters were cast into boiling water. Kamal felt quite indifferent about it.

'It's legitimate money, it has just been manufactured a little more cheaply,' Boris said. It did not take long before Kamal started saying the same thing, and it did not sound strange to his ears.

Kamal's workshop and store were doing well and he had time to attend to some other business. He could count on being involved in further business transactions because of his language skills. Later he would refer to these transactions as 'a little shady'. At the time, Lebanon's economy was booming like never before. Many Arab oil-exporting countries considered Lebanon a safe haven and were investing petrodollars in the country.

Kamal had been approached by a Yugoslav, the director of Trade Exchange, a subsidiary of a large commercial firm called Géfinor. As in his dealings with Boris, he was initially involved as an interpreter, but soon the director got him involved in a deal between the Lebanese government, the firm and the United

Nations. The UN was planning to invest twenty million dollars in a project that would help the Lebanese government develop its agriculture and fishing industries. The money was supposed to subsidise the purchase of two thousand tractors, two ships for the fishing fleet and training for fishermen. The UN was willing to pay for this, on condition that the tractors were purchased from a company called Massey Ferguson. Kamal soon began to understand how politics work. The UN is financed by its member countries. Yugoslavia was a member and paid its contribution in dinars. As currency, dinars were not worth much in international trade. To support Lebanon, the UN had asked Yugoslavia to pay its contribution in kind. Because the Yugoslavs were licensed to build tractors by Massey Ferguson under the name IMT, the Lebanese now had to do business with the country whose language Kamal spoke.

Kamal requested the catalogues and specifications from Industryia Masina I. Traktoru of Belgrade. The director of Trade Exchange suggested they travel to Yugoslavia together and pay a visit to the factory. To his regret, Kamal had to admit he did not have a passport and would not be allowed to travel. They were forced to prepare the application on the basis of the documents they had received by post. A few weeks later, the director managed to get Kamal a laissez-passer for Yugoslavia in his name, pointing out that he might need it when the deal was done. He and the director visited the UN and presented their proposal. The UN agreed, Yugoslavia consented and the Trade Exchange's remuneration was agreed. Kamal received five thousand dollars for what had seemed a very simple job.

'That would be ridiculous, are you really going to let this get in the way?' Kamal said to the Minister of Agriculture. The final stumbling block in the deal with the UN was Lebanon itself.

Although the development project would do the country good, the minister was making trouble. A bribe had to be paid to get things moving. The Minister of Foreign Affairs had agreed to a remuneration of fifty thousand dollars, but the Minister of Agriculture wanted double that.

'I don't understand. You have a good income as a minister, you own several houses and a factory. All this is just a bonus!'

'Don't talk to me like that,' the minister said.

'I'm afraid I have to, because what you want is impossible. This is only about the initial shipment of fifty tractors. If you want a commission of a hundred thousand dollars for these, how much will you want for two thousand tractors?'

The answer was still no. Kamal left the ministry having failed in his quest. Shortly afterwards, he was summoned by the Minister of Foreign Affairs.

'I received a phone call from my colleague at Agriculture and he told me what the two of you discussed. He also told me you have no manners.'

'I was absolutely not out of order,' Kamal answered. 'I had to be clear with him. If you offer him a handful of grain, he will want a kilo.'

'Listen, Kamal. The president listens to him and he will not consent to the project if he tells him not to.'

Kamal looked at him.

'Would you accept the fifty grand?'

'For me, nothing changes. If he accepts, I will too.'

A week later, Kamal had calmed down and he had channelled his anger into a plan of action. He knew a date had been set for a cocktail party at the Yugoslav embassy to celebrate the deal. Both the ministers had been invited and so was the UN. The Yugoslavs and the UN were not aware that the deal was being jeopardised by the Lebanese government. The date was drawing closer and Kamal was hoping to make use of this fact. The government needed to make a decision before the party. Kamal managed to get half an hour with the Prime Minister of Lebanon, Saeb Salam. He was hoping to convince Salam to make a decision. He summarised the situation and the Prime Minister laughed.

'We can't do anything without the consent of the Minister of Agriculture. If I were to get involved, I would be condoning illegal practices by my ministers.'

'But that's the way things are done in this country, isn't it? Sometimes the machine needs to be oiled a little, it is what the country was built on,' Kamal responded.

'I can't help you. If this minister sees fit to earn fifty or a hundred grand somewhere, I don't want to know about it. And Kamal,' the Prime Minister had added, 'we never had this conversation.'

The deal was off.

~

'You can never tell what they're thinking.' This was Kamal's problem with women. He was attracted to them but at the same time he had difficulty understanding them. He would enjoy the company of a woman, but he would always quickly decide it would not be for life.

Mimo Halaby was beautiful. With her long dark hair and dark eyes, she was a typical Arabian beauty. She was three years younger than Kamal. He had met her at a club in Beirut. Mimo was a child of liberal Lebanon, and therefore different from most other women. She was free and independent, had a job, made her own money and had her own place. They enjoyed each other's company and after a while she had practically moved in with him.

They both worked hard and Kamal took good care of her. After work, he would pick up some groceries or take-out. Initially all was well, but after a while he started to grow annoyed by her behaviour. She never offered to pay for food and kept her money to herself. As soon as he noticed this, it started to bother him, but he avoided conflict.

He smoked unfiltered cigarettes, she smoked filtered Marlboros. One day, Kamal had run out of cigarettes and took one from her pack on the table. Mimo was returning from the kitchen and saw what he did.

'Excuse me, those are mine!'

'Oh, come on,' said Kamal, 'I've just run out.'

'Why didn't you buy an extra pack?'

Kamal did not reply, but nor did he forget the incident. Mimo had no idea her response had sealed their fate. Next day they visited friends, a family just outside Beirut. They received a large basket of produce from the garden: fruit, vegetables, potatoes and figs. On their way back, Kamal lied about having to go away for a few days on business and said it would be better if Mimo stayed at her own home. He said they would see each other afterwards and he gave her the fruit and vegetables. He was planning to end their relationship and considered the basket a parting gift. After a few days, she called him. He did not answer. Weeks later, she came to his office at the store.

'Kamal, where were you? Why haven't you answered my messages? You're here, but you didn't come over. What's going on?'

'Your world is not for me,' Kamal answered tactlessly. 'Your attitude is too different from mine. We have to call it a day.'

She came to his door later, but he did not let her in. Later, much later, he realised he had missed his chance. Not for love, but for a passport. He should have married Mimo and acquired Lebanese citizenship. It was not something he had considered at the time. Lebanon was full of refugees from all four corners of the world. Everybody was doing deals and the few rules that were in place were applied only casually. Even without a passport, he had access to schools, bank accounts and permits.

'Kamal, do you know any freemasons?' Boris Bosinov asked one day. Kamal knew a man who traded in jewellery who wore a ring with the freemason's symbol engraved on it. That was all he knew, he had never really looked into what it meant. Boris told him he belonged to a freemason's lodge in Bulgaria and that his membership had helped him at several crucial moments in his life.

'Could you introduce me to him?' Bosinov wanted to know.

'I'll ask him.'

The ring shone brightly and Kamal, who was visiting the merchant, took his first good look at the symbol on the ring, the masonic square and compasses.

'That ring you are wearing, can I ask what it means?'

'I'm a freemason and this is how others recognise me. Some wear a pin with the symbol on it.'

'And the symbol itself?'

The trader explained to him that the compasses were the symbol for the mind, while the square symbolised matter. In the image there is a connection between the instruments that symbolises harmony between opposites: between active and passive, heaven and earth, man and woman.

Kamal explained that he needed an introduction for someone who wanted to join a lodge in Beirut.

'We will have to get to know him first,' said the merchant.

'Of course, that's no problem,' Kamal answered.

He received an address and a short letter of introduction. Out of curiosity, he visited the address before getting back to Boris about it. It was a house with a gate beyond which was a small room with a reception window. He was given a brochure and told to read the information and then come back. Kamal was fascinated by what he read and went to the university library to do some research of his own into freemasonry. Leonardo da Vinci had been a freemason, as had Voltaire, Mozart and Goethe. Kamal discovered a world of concepts he could relate to. He read the words and felt like he could have written them himself. The ideas about tolerance, brotherhood and mutual respect were all his own.

'Boris, I can introduce you to the freemasons.'

Boris was grateful and asked Kamal to go with him as his interpreter. That was exactly what Kamal had been hoping for. Kamal made the appointment and together they went to the house. It soon became clear that there was also a lodge there. The interview actually turned out to be a kind of membership vote. Boris had been a member before and was immediately admitted into the order. Kamal was invited to become an apprentice and to be introduced into the world of freemasonry.

Sadeta had always been a strong, proud woman. She ruled over her husband and son. But her personality slowly began to change as her disease progressed. In 1971, the first signs of paralysis became apparent, laying waste to her independence. She was impulsive and expected those around her to cater to her every whim.

'My mother was a dictator,' Kamal would later say, 'she had a good heart but she had to be in charge.' Kamal could not know exactly how his mother was feeling and had trouble seeing things from her perspective. 'I know she was a beautiful woman who was slowly declining, and she was fighting a difficult fight.'

He spent more and more of his time taking care of his mother. The store was up and running, and he did not always need to be there. Kamal felt that it was his duty to support Sadeta, mostly because he did not want his father to have to stop working.

After a few months, it became harder for Kamal to respond to all of his mother's demands. He decided to get some help. A friend of his had an agency where he could hire a woman to help them out. An Egyptian woman came to take care of his mother.

'I can't keep working here, it's too hard for me,' the woman said after only five days.

Kamal did not understand and asked her to elaborate.

'It's too much' was all she would say.

Kamal went to the agency and told his friend.

'Kamal, you have to tell me something, I'm asking you as a friend,' said the agent.

'What do you want to know?'

'Did you touch her, Kamal?'

'Of course I didn't touch her,' Kamal said indignantly.

'But you should touch her, Kamal, she wants you to. That is why she left. She would have stayed if you had.'

Kamal could not imagine that was true. Only later did he understand that the agency's main business was finding a suitable marriage partner. Although most of the women were young, usually under thirty, they were no longer considered eligible candidates for marriage. Girls got married at fifteen, sixteen years old in the Arab world and these older women, mostly Egyptian, stood little chance of finding a husband.

'Okay, I have more than twenty women on the books. Choose one, take her home and touch her on the first night.'

Kamal now looked at the women with different eyes. He saw one he liked. She had beautiful eyes and she did not turn them away when he looked at her. He explained to her that he would like her to take care of his mother. She agreed and they negotiated her pay.

'If you want peace, Kamal, do what a man has to do,' his friend advised as he left. Kamal took the woman home, where she set about taking care of his mother. The house had a winter garden with a fountain and on the first night, when his mother was asleep and Kamal was sitting out there smoking, the Egyptian carer came over to him.

'Are you tired, Nebija?' he asked.

'No.'

'Good. Come sit with me and have a cigarette.'

They talked about his mother, about Nebija's life, about where she came from, her way of life and eventually, almost automatically, he took her to his bedroom and did what his friend had advised.

'I have done what I had to do, as a man,' he told his friend.

Kamal wondered if this woman would leave after a few days too, but she stayed. After a few months, Nebija told him she was pregnant.

'We shall see,' was all he said and immediately left for the bazaar in the city, not far from his store. He looked for an old man he had visited before to buy medicinal herbs and various sorts of tea for his mother.

'I have a problem.'

'Tell me all about it,' the old man said invitingly.

'My wife is pregnant and I don't know how we are going to manage,' Kamal lied. 'We already have five children and I can't take care of them all. Can you help me? I just don't make enough money.'

'I will see what I can do for you,' said the man and called for his son to bring him two hundred grammes of certain herbs. He did not tell Kamal what they were but told him to make tea from the one, and tablets with the other.

'Get her to drink the tea and take a tablet with each sip. She will have to be brave because it stinks and the taste is foul.'

Kamal went home, prepared the herbs and called for Nebija. She cried, drank the tea and swallowed the tablets. Kamal smoked a cigarette and gave her one. After three puffs, she had had enough. That night she shivered, vomited and bled. She lost the baby, and Kamal was relieved.

Nebija lived with the Kojadin family for over two years. She stayed until 1973, when the Yom Kippur War between Israel and Egypt began and she wanted to go home, to her family. She promised to return after the war.

Meanwhile, Kamal sold his business. Without Nebija it was impossible for him to divide his time between work and taking care of his mother. On top of that, business was bad. The mood in Lebanon started to become restless. Militia groups who felt they were discriminated against by politicians had started to attack prominent citizens in order to stoke unrest. Slowly, the flourishing economy ground to a halt. Kamal sold the store and the workshop for seventy-five thousand dollars so that he and his parents could buy a house. They moved to a small town called Bhamdoun, more than twenty kilometres from Beirut. It was a popular summer residence for people from the capital. At an altitude of eleven hundred metres, it was a lot cooler at that time of year. Wealthy people, in particular, would go there to escape the heat of the city. Their new home was close to that of the Najjar family, his father's employer.

Forty days later, Nebija came back, as promised. She helped Kamal until the following year, when his mother died on 5 August. Sadeta Kojadin-Adinovic was buried in Bhamdoun.

Kamal's father was sixty-four years of age when his wife died. It was a huge shock for him, and Kamal found it hard to see his father cry. Saïm had health issues himself. A few years earlier, in 1972, he had developed a pain in his lower back. He visited a German doctor he knew and trusted. The X-rays showed cancer in the spine and he was given medication that would slow down the disease, but would not stop it.

'How long does he have, doctor?' Kamal had asked.

'In his condition, I would say about four years,' the doctor answered. He turned out to be right.

'Do you still have contacts in Egypt?' one of his father's visitors asked. The two men had announced their arrival, and although his father was trying to keep his past in the past, he had agreed to receive them. He knew one of them from the war. The man, who was from Bosnia, had also worked in intelligence, with a unit in the harbour town of Split, where a barber's shop served as a cover for an espionage ring. He had a Frenchman with him who had worked as a representative of the company that manufactured Mirage jet fighters. Saïm soon understood what the visit was about. After losing the Yom Kippur War of 1973, Egypt was in dire need of combat aircraft and weapons. Kuwait had ordered a number of Mirages from the French and the Bosnian man told him he knew the aircraft were being secretly sold on to Egypt. The men saw a business opportunity, selling weapons from Yugoslavia to Egypt. They were looking for someone who knew both countries and spoke both languages. Kamal listened to the conversation from the kitchen and felt the tension rising in the living room. His father was being intimidated by the Bosnian, who had started off the conversation so amiably. He was now threatening to discredit Saïm by revealing his past if he refused to help them. Kamal stepped into the room and boldly interrupted the conversation.

'Gentlemen, you have no business here. You are asking about things that do not concern you, they are my father's business. This conversation is over, you can go now. We don't like spies round here.'

His father was surprised by his resolute demeanour, but he nodded in agreement. The men got up and left the house without another word.

~

Boris Bosinov had suddenly reappeared. Kamal had not heard from him in a long time and had no idea where he had been.

'Where have you been all this time, what kind of job are you doing?' Kamal had asked.

'I'm working with the Palestinians.'

'Doing what?'

'I'm working for them in a camp.'

Suddenly it dawned on him. 'You're not involved with weapons, are you, Boris?'

'Never mind, don't ask me about it,' he answered, and Kamal knew he was right.

The Palestinian camp for refugees in Lebanon was called Sabra. There were underground spaces there where the Palestinians were preparing their campaign of resistance against Israel, and Boris was involved in some business that would not stand the light of day. In the run-up to the civil war there was a lively trade in all kinds of useful items. Boris asked him if he had any time to spare. Since he had sold the store, Kamal had plenty of time, and soon he had a thriving new business. Although it was quite shady, the nature of this business intrigued him. He traded in cutlery, jungle boots, small weapons and munitions and in jerrycans. The weapons and goods were intended for all kinds of groups in Lebanon.

He had shifted his boundaries before in order to make money. Once, when he still had his store and his mother was still alive, he had been approached by one of his upper-class contacts who had asked him to deliver a suitcase full of jewels to a hotel in Istanbul. Kamal had explained that he did not have a passport and he could therefore not just go abroad. He had been told that was not a problem. He had been offered ten thousand dollars and shortly afterwards he was on his way to Istanbul with a false passport. He delivered the suitcase and flew back the next day without ever feeling guilty about it. In his eyes, it was simply how business was done in Lebanon. Once or twice a year he was asked to go on a little trip with a suitcase full of jewels or gold. And so the man without a passport flew to Istanbul, Marseille, Madrid and even Chicago, each time under a false identity.

Kamal was having the time of his life. He bought the latest fashions, dined at the best restaurants, had fleeting relationships with several women and drove around in a car. He had money and he spent it. The false passports did not really help him, because the expiry date was never far from the day he travelled.

'This country is in trouble,' Kamal said to his father. Saïm had turned away from politics a long time ago and the only thing he did apart from work was keeping up with his hobbies, breeding songbirds and rereading *Thus Spoke Zarathustra* by Nietzsche. It was his father's go-to book which explained the theory of the 'übermensch' that the Nazis had made their own. By now, Kamal knew his father interpreted it differently. Saïm had always told him that every person had a responsibility to constantly improve themselves and to work at being a better person, and that was why Nietzsche had written the book.

Although Kamal had no interest in politics either, he realised that the political climate in Lebanon was changing.

'Don't worry, we will see,' said his father, who wholeheartedly trusted his employer.

Old Najjar's company had been taken over by his son and daughter, and the son was a prominent member of the business community in Beirut. He was also a member of the Druze, a small religious group with a lot of political influence, and he was in a position to use his contacts to protect people. Therefore, Saïm was counting on him. Kamal and his father could not escape the mounting tension, which was especially palpable as they travelled home from their jobs in Beirut. They often found it difficult to make their way there, and were forced to take detours because of fighting in the streets of the city. New checkpoints appeared every day, some of them on their journey home, which was a strategically important route to the Bekaa Valley. At one time they had to pass at least twenty checkpoints. Large concrete blocks formed barricades that they had to weave their way through. Paramilitary groups with automatic guns checked every passenger. Every group had its own checkpoints and it was unclear which ones they would encounter and how much of a risk they were taking.

One day, a few kilometres from home, they were stopped at a new barricade. Armed soldiers dressed as civilians asked them for their papers, then arrested them and took them into custody. In fact, they had been kidnapped by Christian militia who were after Muslims. They were taken to the Catholic part of Beirut and held in a school full of armed soldiers in uniform. The atmosphere was quite relaxed and Kamal even got permission to go and buy some food for himself and his father at the store on the opposite side of the road. He never thought of attempting an escape, because they had told him they would hurt his father if he tried anything. He returned with a fried chicken, bread, milk and a bottle of ouzo.

'What's this? You're a Muslim, aren't you?' the officer said when he saw the ouzo.

'I feel more connected to God than to his rules and my father and I like to drink. Our faith is something I discuss with God,' Kamal had answered.

The officer liked his answer and had a glass of ouzo with his prisoners. After eating and waiting for a few hours, Kamal knocked on the door to the room where the soldiers were.

'Commander, could I use the phone?'

'Why? Who do you want to call?'

'My mother,' Kamal lied, 'she needs to know we are here.'

He was given permission and hesitated before dialling the number. It was fortunate he did so, as the officer left the room while Kamal called Najjar's son. He was acquainted with a general in the Lebanese army, also a Druze. Kamal explained where they were being held prisoner. A few hours later, four tanks drove through the streets of Beirut and took up positions around the school where the Phalangists were hiding. They demanded the release of the two prisoners. Shortly afterwards, Kamal and his father climbed on board one of the tanks which took them to the offices of Najjar and Sons, just like a taxi. Radjer Najjar was waiting for them.

'Here's the key to our apartment above the office. You can stay there until the situation has calmed down a little.'

For three months they lived in the company apartment, close to the port. They never managed to return to their house in Bhamdoun to collect their belongings. Looters were marauding through the streets of Beirut, and they raided Kamal's shop. It was decided that Kamal's father should leave for Lausanne. After Zagreb, Cairo and Damascus, this would be the fourth time Saïm had had to leave everything behind. Later, they heard that the house in Bhamdoun was being used as a radio station by the Kataeb party, a Phalangist faction.

Halfway through January 1976 Kamal's father left for Switzerland. A few days earlier, Kamal had already left for the safety of Damascus, leaving behind the country of his youth and many happy memories.

1976, LAUSANNE

The message about his father's death had reached him in Damascus. Kamal realised their goodbye in Beirut had been the last time he had seen his father alive.

He arranged the few documents he had on his hotel bed: the laissez-passer for Switzerland, the temporary permit that would allow him to stay in the country for a little longer and the laissez-passer for Yugoslavia that he had received when he had done business with Industryia Masina I. Traktoru, the Belgrade-based company that was to supply tractors to Lebanon. He felt as though he had played all his cards. He looked at the documents and realised he was looking at a losing hand.

Kamal was alone. He did not know what was in store for him and he no longer had a sounding board. His father had always been his adviser and he missed him now more than ever. He had a decision to make and, looking at his cards, he decided his best option was to return to the country of his birth. His roots were there, his parents' family still lived there and his hopes lay with them. He did not want much, just a place where he would feel at home and a few people to connect with. He knew a man there called Ahmed

Dervisevic who owned a restaurant and a boarding house. He was one of the sons of the family his parents had befriended in Rome. Kamal had played with him and his brother, Ali. He had met Ali again in Beirut. He was also working for Géfinor, the trading company involved in the tractor deal, and they had become friends. That too was a reason for his decision, this old friendship with the Dervisevic family. He was sure they would help him. And of course money was a factor. He estimated he could exchange his Swiss francs for a good pile of dinars and that at least he would have a modest capital to start up a little business in Yugoslavia.

'My father would have killed me if he knew I was going to Yugoslavia,' Kamal would later say, but still he decided to go.

By the end of the summer, Kamal was on his way to Zagreb, the city of his birth. His parents had left the place over thirty years ago, and Kamal was returning by the same route. Like his parents back then, he carried all his belongings with him. Getting into the country was no problem. His travel pass allowed him to cross the border quite easily. And so Kamal entered Yugoslavia, the country he would later call 'camp Yugoslavia'. In later life, he often recalled this moment. When he left his children behind, when he was threatened by the Serbs and had to flee, when he was working as a solitary shepherd, and as he wandered the streets of Sarajevo. Every time he would tell his friends about his biggest mistake.

He did not realise he was walking into a prison, a state that in time would be like a detention camp. A country he was allowed to enter, but that would not allow him to leave again.

He walked through the streets of Zagreb looking for a building his parents had described to him, the skyscraper where they had lived on the eighth floor at the end of the war. He had no idea where it was and a considerable number of buildings were taller than eight floors by now. He asked a number of elderly people in the streets, hoping they would remember what had been the tallest building in Zagreb thirty years before, but no one could help. The place where he had spent the first months of his life turned out to be untraceable. He exchanged his francs for dinars and left the bank with a large stack of banknotes. He drank a cup of coffee at the Dolac market, not far from the cathedral. The lively market with the multicoloured fruits, vegetables and flowers reminded him of Beirut. It was just a flicker of recognition; there was not much else about the city that felt familiar. It soon became clear there was nothing left for him in Zagreb.

1976 - 1980, OPATIJA

It took half a day to get from Zagreb to Rijeka, the most important port on the coast of Yugoslavia, by train. In Beirut, when he had befriended Ali Dervisevic, they had talked about his family and Kamal remembered that his brother owned a restaurant in Opatija called the Citadel. Kamal pinned all his hopes on him. He took a slow train to the small station at Opatija-Matulji. Carrying all his possessions in two suitcases, he walked out of the station and took a taxi to the centre. As they descended towards Kvarner Bay, Kamal enjoyed the stunning views of the beautiful coast and the blue sea. It was the sea that made him feel he had made the right decision. It reminded him of all the times he had spent at Ramblat Al Bayda, Beirut's beach, where he had swum in the Mediterranean. When the taxi dropped him off in the centre of Opatija, he asked around for the Citadel. It did not ring any bells with anyone. At the tourist information office, he was told the restaurant was in Ika, a small harbour town just south of Opatija. Kamal took another taxi to Ika. The Citadel turned out to be situated a little higher up in the hills, and Kamal regretted sending the taxi away. Now he would have to drag his suitcases up the hill. Twenty minutes later he spotted the restaurant.

'Kamal, is that really you? Where did you come from?'

Naturally, Ahmed was surprised to see him there. Kamal had to explain who he was. Ahmed had only ever seen Kamal as a child in Rome, but he knew all about him from the stories he had heard from his brother Ali about Beirut. Kamal was warmly received and he felt welcome and at ease. He was introduced to family and friends. Everyone spoke his mother tongue and he felt completely at home with the sound, the language of his childhood. There had not been any contact between them for a long time, and they knew nothing about his mother's death, his father's illness or the period he had spent in Switzerland. Kamal's situation soon became clear to them: he was alone, without valid papers and without a home. Ahmed offered him a place in the kitchens and a bed in a small room on the upper floor of the boarding house. Kamal was grateful; he was starting a new life.

'There is not much we can do for you,' the police officer told Kamal. 'You have a laissez-passer for our country, but nothing else. You can only stay here if somebody is willing to vouch for you.'

'I will vouch for him, that's not a problem,' Ahmed said, 'but he needs valid papers. He was born here.'

Kamal and Ahmed were sent away after Kamal had left his personal details with them, and he was assured that the police would look into the matter.

Two weeks later, Kamal received a request to report to the police station again. Ahmed went with him. This time, the atmosphere was a lot less amicable. The officer only spoke to Ahmed and ignored Kamal. It seemed he did not want anything to do with him.

'Do you even know who his father is?' he asked Ahmed, who had only known Saïm Kojadin as a child in Rome. He remembered the man who had often visited his parents as a kind uncle. This was the first time he had heard the word Ustaše in relation to Kamal's father.

'Kojadin is a traitor to his people and a war criminal and this man is his son.'

That was above all how people regarded Kamal – as his father's son.

'Your father was an asshole, Kamal, even if you don't see it like that, he really was.'

Kamal was standing there, facing a man who clearly harboured a personal hatred of anyone who was in any way connected with his country's Nazi past. This was what his father had warned him about and at that moment it became clear to him that he was persona non grata. Here, he was considered a man with a dark history, a fascist, an enemy of the Yugoslavian people, because of the role his father had played.

'A son of the Ustaše' the officer had literally called him and Kamal now realised how deep the hatred between different groups ran here and how difficult it was going to be to find somebody who would be willing to help him get his papers.

Kamal soon got used to his new life. He worked in the Dervisevic family's kitchen and in the vegetable garden. He learned fast and after a few months he was able to prepare most of the dishes. The goldsmith and merchant had become a cook. He had refined his palate in Lebanon and he even managed to improve the dishes with all kinds of fresh herbs and blends of spices that he created himself. Ahmed was very pleased with Kamal's work. He was getting more customers because the word was spreading about his new Lebanese cook. Kamal played his new role with zeal, but that did not mean he had lost track of his real goals.

'I simply can't do without you here, Kamal', said Ahmed.

'Why is that? Six months ago you barely knew I existed!' Kamal cried.

Tensions between the two men were running high. Kamal had said he was going to leave in a week to search for his family on his father's side and although Ahmed understood why, he was now thinking only of his personal losses.

'We're booked full almost every evening, it's going so well. I can't find a replacement as good as you in such a short time.'

Kamal hesitated. He owed a lot to Ahmed, who had been so hospitable to him and who had given him the chance to learn a new profession. On the other hand, he had been working day and night for food and lodgings for months. He decided to give in a little and settled for a compromise; he would stay until after the high season.

By the end of 1977 Kamal was on his way to Travnik, the place where his father had been born. He had one suitcase full of clothes and an olive-green Samsonite briefcase with all kinds of papers that he had found among his father's things in Switzerland, and which he thought might be useful. He also had a letter whose contents he was not entirely sure of. It was in a sealed envelope and he had received it from a man who had eaten at the Citadel. Kamal had cooked for a group of twenty-five people and one of them had been so pleased, he had asked for the cook afterwards. Kamal had had a conversation with him and given the man a brief account of his life so far.

'If there is anything I can do for you, tell me,' the man said and when Kamal told him he was planning to search for his family, the man had made him an offer.

'The mayor of Travnik is a friend of my father's. I could write a letter of recommendation for you.'

Naturally, Kamal had taken him up on the offer and, with the letter in his pocket, he travelled to Travnik via Rijeka and checked in to a hotel. The man had told him he should report to the registrar's office and ask for the manager of the department. Kamal did so and the manager soon came to see him.

'Someone asked me to give you this letter.'

The man opened the envelope and laughed. Without asking Kamal anything, he said, 'We can help you and get you what you need.'

Kamal was happy. The letter had clearly worked. The manager called his secretary. 'Bring me the register of births for 1910 and let Mr Kojadin have a look.'

Kamal was shown the archives and soon he was browsing through the lists of names. He looked through it again, leafing back and forth through the book. The name Saïm Kojadin was not there. He searched the pages again, but he did not find his father's name. He did, however find a Kojadin, born on 27 February 1910. It was his father's birthday, and he knew this had to be his father. Yet this Kojadin's first name was not Saïm, but Zvonimir: a Christian name, not a name Muslims would ever give their child. A little later, Kamal was certain. At the bottom of the page, there was a handwritten note that Zvonimir Kojadin had married Sadeta Adinovic in August 1941. His father, a Christian? Kamal was surprised and confused. He asked the secretary for a copy and he went back to the manager and thanked him. It was a memorable day. His father had never been very talkative, had never told him anything about his Christian background. For as long as he lived, he had known his father as a Muslim and he had been raised as such. Only now did Kamal see things as they really were. He had never wondered why he had been sent to be educated at a convent as a young boy in Egypt. He had never given much thought to the fact that his education with the Jesuits in Aintoura had been in the Christian district of Keserwan. He had always assumed his father had simply chosen the best possible education for him. Only now did he realise that his father, a devout Muslim in his eyes, had chosen these schools because of his Catholic background.

Kamal smoothed out the copy of the register that he had crumpled up in anger before. He found his father's silence for all those years particularly troubling and he needed some time to think about what this meant for him.

Among his father's papers he had found a photograph of his father with his sister Vera and her three sons. Back in his hotel room he searched through the Samsonite again for the picture so he could take another look. There was his father, still very young, together with a stern-looking woman and three boys. He intended to search for his aunt Vera and he thought it would be best to go to the police first.

The following day he crossed the street to the police station and asked to see the commander at the desk.

'I am Kamal Kojadin, son of Zvonimir, who was born here.'

'Okay, what do you want?'

Kamal showed him the picture and said, 'I am looking for my aunt and I have no idea if she is still alive, or if she lives in this area. Do you think you could help me?'

Contrary to his earlier experiences with the Yugoslavian police, the man seemed quite forthcoming.

'Okay, we will see what we can do. How can we get in touch with you?'

'I'm staying at Hotel Travnik,' Kamal answered.

'That's easy, we'll call you when we have something.'

The next morning at eight o'clock, the hotel reception called his room to tell him there was a police officer waiting for him in the lobby. Kamal was delighted with the quick response. He took the elevator down and walked into the hall. It turned out there were in fact three men waiting for him. One of them was an officer from Travnik and the other two were from an organization Kamal could not later recall, although they did introduce themselves.

'Can we sit down somewhere?' one of the men asked. Kamal was surprised by the question, as there were plenty of seats in the otherwise deserted lobby. He pointed to one of the seating areas and they sat down. Kamal was asked all the usual questions: where he came from, what his background was and what he was doing here. They seemed particularly interested in the fact that he was Zvonimir's son.

'Where is your father now?'

Kamal told them his father had passed away and was buried in Switzerland. As they questioned him about it, he noticed they were suspicious.

'Do you have anything in your room?' Before Kamal could answer them they continued, 'Can we see it?'

Kamal knew it would be pointless to object and he led the men to his room and showed them his suitcase and his father's Samsonite.

'Can we take a look inside?' It was not exactly a question.

'Why not?' answered Kamal. 'I haven't got anything to hide.'

They opened his suitcase and thumbed through the papers.

'Could we take these papers back to the station for further investigation?'

This too sounded more like a command than a question.

'That's fine, as long as I get everything back. They are my father's documents.' 'Let me know if you find anything you think is important,' he called after them as they left with his father's little briefcase.

The following morning Kamal again received a request to come down to the lobby. At the desk, he was told to report to the police station. He crossed the street and was taken to a small interrogation room. Shortly afterwards, two men who did not look like police officers walked in.

'What does this address mean to you?' one of them asked as he slid a note in his father's handwriting over to him. It was an address in Canada. It did not mean anything to Kamal. Then he was shown an address in Los Angeles and a name, another of his father's notes. The address did not ring any bells, but the name was familiar. He remembered his father had corresponded a lot with this Alois Anich, but he told them none of it meant anything to him.

'My father had plenty of foreign contacts because of his job at Najjar's. I assume it has something to do with that. I took those papers from his office in Switzerland.'

The men were mostly interested in the names from earlier times, the names of his father's friends during the war. They asked about Kamal's beliefs and opinions too, but he managed to avoid the topic of politics. He had learned from his father that your beliefs could get you into trouble. It soon became clear to them that Kamal did not know much and they accepted that his father had never wanted to talk about the past, and that Kamal was now merely looking for his roots and his family here in Yugoslavia. Much later, Kamal found out that Alois Anich was an alias of Andrija Artukovic, the former NDH Minister of Foreign Affairs. This fascist war criminal was known as the butcher of the Balkans and he is estimated to have been responsible for over a million deaths.

Kamal was free to go. They returned the green Samsonite and its contents, but not the addresses his father had noted down.

Early the next afternoon, two men again announced their arrival at the desk of Hotel Travnik. Kamal left his hotel room and walked into the lobby. There he met the police officer he had spoken to the day before together with a man he did not know, who introduced himself as his cousin. Kamal immediately felt sympathetic towards the man. This was one of the three boys portrayed in his father's picture of aunt Vera and for the first time in his life he was meeting an actual relative. He felt a huge wave of joy come over him. Now the tide would surely turn, his life would start anew.

'Come home with me, you can get to know my wife and my mother.'

Kamal was filled with hope and anticipation. A little later his cousin took him to his home on the outskirts of Travnik. There he met his cousin's wife. Aunt Vera was still at work and they drank tea as they waited for her. Although the conversation was slightly awkward and mostly concerned the couple's experiences as young parents, the atmosphere was good. The cousin kept an eye on the garden path and when his mother appeared, he rushed to the door.

'Kemo is here, Zvonko's son,' Kamal heard him say. 'He has come to visit you and get to know you.'

Aunt Vera entered the room, but did not come over to greet him. She lifted one of her grandchildren in her arms and hung back a little, sitting down with her back slightly turned to him. Kamal did not understand what was going on. He felt uncomfortable as the atmosphere in the small living room quickly changed. His cousin did his best to keep the conversation going. Kamal had been given a fresh cup of tea but with the mounting tension he had not taken a sip. He gathered up all his courage and asked what was going on.

Before his cousin could answer him, aunt Vera said with a firm voice, from the other side of the room, 'You do not look anything like my brother. You are not family.'

Her tone was so stern and direct that he did not dare ask for an explanation. He was completely taken aback by her comment. He had counted on a warm welcome and now his existence was being flatly denied by his aunt. Feeling insulted and humiliated, Kamal got up and walked to the door. At the same time, his cousin stood up and accompanied him along the garden path.

'I'm sorry if I'm not welcome here. I shouldn't have come at all.'

'It all has to do with your mother, Kamal,' his cousin explained. 'She was a Muslim and your father was a Catholic, and it caused a lot of trouble in the family.'

Kamal looked at him and said, 'But that was thirty years ago.'

'I know, Kemo, I know,' his cousin answered, gesturing that he did not understand it either.

'Please take me back to the hotel.'

His cousin nodded and took him back by car. After this meeting, Kamal had no more contact with his father's side of the family. He was hurt and his pride kept him from making an effort to connect with them and so he lost his chance to substantiate his paper-thin identity. The love between his parents had led his father to renounce his Catholic faith. He had chosen to become a Muslim; it was the only way he could marry Sadeta. Since then, his father had called himself Saïm Kojadin and Kamal was brought up to be a Muslim. Everything he had always taken for granted seemed so different now. His father's name turned out to be an assumed one and the family bond Kamal had been hoping to find turned out not to exist. The journey to Travnik and his five nights at the hotel had cost him a lot of money. He had come with great expectations, and after this rejection his disappointment was all the greater. A longer stay would have been pointless, so he returned to Opatija.

'It was a mistake to come to Yugoslavia, Ahmed,' he told his friend. 'I should never have done it. I thought I would find my roots here, and I did, but they turned out to be rotten.'

In Nova Gorica, a small town in what is now Slovenia, there is a road just behind the train station, parallel to the tracks. Beyond that is the Italian border. Kamal had heard that people had managed to escape Yugoslavia this way. He had already tried to acquire a false passport. In Lebanon he had had several for his illegal business trips, but it was different in Yugoslavia. Money was not the problem, he had enough left to buy false documents, but he did not know the right people. He did not know who he could trust. Indeed, apart from the Dervisevic family, he did not know anybody. He also got the impression that people did not easily trust him. He was a stranger, a foreigner, a Lebanese cook. It is not what you know but who you know. That had been his father's saying, and it was being confirmed now. In Lebanon, Kamal had had contacts in the highest circles, yet here in Yugoslavia he did not know anyone.

It was late 1978 and, feeling desperate, he had decided to try to illegally cross the border to Italy in the hope of turning his life around. His plan was to take a bus to Trieste. Someone had told him the best place to try, and where the bus stop was. It was a dreary November day. Getting to Nova Gorica by train proved easy. Soon evening fell and with nothing but some hand luggage, Kamal started to look for the place to cross the border. He was soon picked up by plainclothes police officers, however, and his adventure quickly came to an end.

Kamal blamed fate for his bad luck. His cell was cold and empty. He was occupied by one single thought: so many people were trying to escape their past and their identities, while he was simply desperate to have one. Not just to have a name, but to have proof of his existence. Only then would he truly exist, only then would he truly be alive.

'Passports are only good for annoying honest folks, and aiding in the flight of rogues,' he had once read in Jules Verne's famous book *Around the World in 80 Days*. It seemed to him that the opposite was true. After he had spent a few days in the cell, two officers escorted Kamal to the railway station. They watched as the train left for Opatija.

Kamal had worked for his friend Ahmed in the Citadel for almost two years. He had had enough of it, and now felt trapped. There was always more work to be done and he could not imagine that working in the kitchen, the orchard and the vegetable garden would be his entire life from now on. This was not the place for him. Freedom was calling and he decided to leave. Ahmed was about to lose a good worker and he tried to talk him round. But he did understand Kamal and as a friend urged him to find something that would suit him. Kamal was curious about life in Opatija and he decided to move down from the hills above Ika towards the bay to try his luck in town. Unwilling to work in a hotel or restaurant any longer, he decided to offer his services at the many stores that catered to the needs of tourists. After a few attempts, he chanced upon a woman who sold handmade clothing in her small shop. He asked her if she needed a good salesman and, since her talents mostly lay in designing and making clothes, she was willing to give him a try for one season. Her name was Rifeta, an older woman and a good person, Kamal would later recall. She was prepared to pay him three hundred dinars a month. In Kamal's eyes, it was a good salary. It quickly became apparent he would have made more if he worked on commission, because he was a good salesman. At the end of the month he would have no money left, but he kept working. Others asked him why he was not working on commission, as there would not be any work in the winter and he would not have anything to live off. Kamal said he was contented and did not want to start looking for another job, that it was his first year working like this and that he felt free and was enjoying himself. Since Kamal had started working for Rifeta, her shop was doing better than ever. He had a charming smile and, what is more, he had his mother's eye for what looked good on a woman. Rifeta was happy with Kamal working behind her counter.

$\sim$

'Kamal, do you know that woman outside?' Rifeta said. 'She has been looking at you for over ten minutes.'

Kamal looked. She was standing about twenty paces away from him. He did not know her, but she smiled when he looked at her. He got on with his work and did not pay her any more attention. Three customers and almost an hour later he saw she was back, or still there, and she smiled again. Kamal took a better look. She was roughly his age, not particularly beautiful but good-looking enough. Kamal went over and greeted her.

'Don't you want to come into the store?' he asked.

'No, I want to know when you finish work,' she answered in German. It was no trouble at all for Kamal to answer her in her own language.

'At nine o'clock tonight.'

'Right, I will be back then. I want to go for a beer with you.'

She was pleasantly straightforward, and Kamal liked that. He immediately felt sympathetic towards her and he agreed to meet her.

'My name is Monika, by the way,' she called out as she turned and walked away. Again, she flashed a smile that made Kamal look forward to the evening.

A little before nine, she came strolling back. Kamal closed the store and together they walked towards the sea to sit down at a café for a glass of beer.

'So, what is your name?'

'They call me Kemo here,' answered Kamal. 'Where are you from?'

'Austria, Vienna, that's where I live.'

'And what do you do there?'

'I work at a bank.'

And so the conversation continued as they ate together. Kamal soon felt at ease and he decided to ask her a direct question.

'Monika, what do you want? Why did you invite me?'

'I like you,' she answered and gave him another smile. From that moment, Kamal felt like a sort of happiness entered his life. He wondered why it was, the way he always wondered why his life took such unexpected turns. Kamal wanted to pay the bill, but Monika was adamant that she would.

'No, Kemo, I'm paying, I'm the one who invited you. By the way, is that your store you're working at?'

'No, I work for someone else.'

'How much do you earn?' she asked, another straightforward question.

'Three hundred dinars.'

Monika looked him straight in the eye and from her look, he knew she understood exactly what that meant. She knew it was barely enough to live off.

'Where do you live, Kemo?'

'Not far from here.'

'Can I come with you?'

'No, you can't. You really can't.'

'Kemo, why not?'

'It's a small room with a narrow bed with only half a metre of space next to it and a small window. I cannot receive guests there, it is too small for two people.'

Kamal found it easy to be honest with Monika and she appreciated his frank response.

'Would you like to come with me to my room?'

'You know your situation best, you tell me.'

Monika found it a pleasantly compliant answer that implied an unspoken 'yes'. They walked through the streets of Opatija towards the room she had rented. Kamal told her they were close to his place and he pointed out the apartment building where he lived. It turned out Monika was staying in the same building. The rooms on the higher floors, belonging to another landlord, were larger and more luxurious. All the floors shared an entrance.

'I'm going up and I'll leave my door open. Give me a few minutes before you come up.'

Kamal did as she said and quietly went up to her room. That night he stayed with Monika.

'Have you seen your sweetheart?' was the first thing Rifeta asked when he walked into the store the next morning.

'What sweetheart?'

'The woman who stood watching you for over an hour, of course!'

'Oh, her. I met up with her,' Kamal answered casually.

'And?'

'We had a beer.'

'Don't lose that one,' the old lady said.

'Eh, why?'

'A woman who stares at you for an hour, that's a keeper. You must woo her, win her over, this is your chance.'

'Okay, mother,' Kamal answered. He called her that sometimes when she gave him words of advice. It set him thinking. Rifeta had called Monika a 'chance'. He was not in the habit of calculating probabilities. He had not yet given any thought to the fact that a relationship with Monika could be the first step towards acquiring a passport, and an Austrian passport at that. He would have to look into the possibilities of getting a new identity through marriage. But he quickly pushed the thought away. He did not want to start a relationship for that reason. It was just not him.

That evening at nine, Monica came strolling by again. Kamal was just closing up the shop.

'Come, let's go for a drink.'

'Okay, but it's my treat this time.'

Monika consented and they had a beer on a terrace by the little harbour of Opatija, enjoying the warm spring evening.

'How long are you staying?'

'I'll be here for seven more days.'

They were sauntering back towards the apartment building.

'Are you coming over tonight?

Kamal had intended to say he was not sure, but he nodded in agreement. He hesitated, wanting to be just as straightforward as Monika. He sensed she was not just looking for a holiday adventure, that she was serious. And so the seven days passed. They saw each other every day and Kamal felt the connection between them grow. Monika was sweet, smart and good-natured. Her love for him grew and although Kamal's feelings were friendly rather than amorous, he did not want to put a stop to their relationship. It was not calculated, it was just Kamal's way, going along with whatever was happening.

At the end of the week, she left. She was to depart during working hours and Kamal had asked Rifeta for two hours off so he could accompany her to the railway station. They said their goodbyes on the platform.

'Shall I come back next summer, Kamal?'

'That's fine.'

That was all he said. He had intended to use bigger words but, standing there on the platform, it was all he could come up with. Monika gave him one last look, and he did not know what to read into it. He realised he hardly knew her at all. Monika left and did not come back that summer. Kamal was disappointed. He blamed himself for letting her go and was aware that his parting words had been too tepid to strengthen her feelings towards him enough for her to make the journey again.

His hands were red and chafed and at night they itched horribly. The season had passed, Rifeta no longer had any work for him and Kamal had found another job for the winter, cleaning seashells with caustic soda and vinegar. He collected them along the coast, filling buckets, and changed the cleaning agents every few days to bring out the glossiness of the shells.

He had met a man who owned a small workshop where he made and sold figures out of shells. The man could use a hand, he said. Off season, the wages were even lower and Kamal earned only two hundred dinars a month. It was not enough to live properly, but it was just enough to get him through the winter. His new employer also made candles and asked Kamal to sell them for ten dinars apiece. He would be paid on commission. Kamal took a bus to Rijeka, where there were several Christian cemeteries. Lots of Italians would visit one of the cemeteries in Rijeka on All Souls' Day and All Saints' Day. Kozala cemetery contained many graves of Italian soldiers who had died in the First World War. Kamal sold the candles individually and managed to make some money. The short conversations with the Italians and the sounds of their language reminded him of his youth and he decided to try and escape the country once more. In late 1979 he wandered around the harbour of Opatija and boarded a ferry, unseen, as a stowaway. It was a small vessel and he was discovered by the crew before they had even left the harbour and handed over to the police. Once again he was unable to identify himself. He did ask the police to contact the authorities in Opatija and told them they would know who he was. Nobody made a big deal of it, and a few phone calls later Kamal was free to go.

'Kamal, are you there?' The owner of his apartment in Opatija knocked on his door. 'There's someone here to see you.'

Kamal opened the door. It was Monika and he saw in her eyes, in the way she looked at him, that she was in love with him. It made him feel uncomfortable.

'I've come to see you. I tried to forget you, but I can't, Kamal.'

He embraced her, not out of desire, but to hide his own discomfort. She stayed for three days. She had managed to get away from work for a few days. She wanted his love, to connect with him. Although Kamal was still not quite in love with her, his feelings for her started to grow again. He began to feel at ease in her company and enjoyed the attention she gave him during her visit. He felt like fate was playing a game with him, directing him towards a new path in life, that something was about to happen to turn his life around. After three days Monika left again, but before she departed she opened her bag and took out two thousand Austrian shillings.

'I know there's not much work for you right now, Kamal, so I'm sure you could use this.' It was more than his monthly salary and he could certainly do with a little extra in wintertime, but he did not want to make the impression he was in it for money.

'I don't want it, I cannot take your money.'

'You have to take it, Kamal, it's a gift.'

She kept insisting, but he did not accept the money. He took her to the railway station and she left. It was more than love, it had gone beyond that. Monika worshipped him. Every three to four weeks throughout the winter she came to Opatija. Kamal went to work and when he got home in the evenings she was there. They ate in a restaurant overlooking the sea.

'Kamal, let's just go and take a train to Belgrade.'

'Now? Why, what do you want to do there?'

'We'll stay at a hotel and tomorrow morning we'll go to the Austrian embassy to see if we can get you a visa.'

Kamal thought about it and nodded in agreement.

'I want to help you get away from here, I want you to come with me to Austria and get married.

Kamal was not surprised by the proposal. He had skirted around the subject himself because he did not want to seem too calculating. Gradually, the thought of marriage as a means to escape Yugoslavia had entered his mind after Rifeta's words. He had waited for Monika to broach the subject. Now that the moment was here, he felt uneasy for a moment, but he quickly shook off his anxiety.

'I was afraid to ask you, Monika, but I want it very much.' He did not feel quite right answering her like this, yet still he did it. 'Let's take a few days to think it over before we make our journey of hope,' he added.

A few days later they took a night train from Rijeka to Belgrade and visited the embassy. It soon became clear that without any valid papers, without an identity, it was impossible to get a visa. The gate to Austria remained closed.

∽

She had blue eyes, dark eyebrows and beautiful long hair, but Kamal did not notice her good looks. He had approached Smelia about getting a job. Close to his house was a little shop on the boulevard where the beautiful young gipsy sold roughly the same wares as Rifeta. She had a larger assortment though, and Kamal was sure the clothes and other items she stocked would be more attractive to tourists, and that her shop was more likely to have a good turnover because of her location. Kamal saw it as an opportunity to make more money than the summer before. He told her he had worked for Rifeta and asked if she needed a salesman for the summer. She agreed and this time, because he now knew he was a good salesman, he proposed that he work on commission.

Things started out well. The sun was shining, the tourists came and they made a good profit. Kamal and Smelia worked well together and he enjoyed going to work each morning. She was cheerful and they laughed a lot, about the customers, about little things that happened and about the contents of the cash register at the end of each day. In the evenings, he swam in the sea, dined with friends and enjoyed life. It had been a long time since he felt this good.

It was springtime and Monika had come to Opatija again. Kamal's landlord had pointed out the shop on the boulevard to her and a little later they saw each other again. Kamal was happy to see her. As he was still at work, they decided to meet up again that evening. Smelia came up from the back of the store and Kamal introduced Monika to her. Soon, the two women were talking to each other and out of politeness, Monika bought a bottle of perfume.

'Kamal, could you do something for me?' Smelia asked and she told him a pile of clothes had to be taken out to be washed and ironed. This was not unusual. Clothes sometimes had to be washed and ironed before they were fit to be displayed in the store and they always went to the same place. Kamal agreed and took the bundle of clothing. It was a ten-minute walk and it would only take him half an hour to run this errand. He asked Monika to hang around until he got back and give some thought to what she would like to do that evening, where she would like to go for dinner and whether she would maybe like to go dancing afterwards. As soon as he had gone, Smelia opened fire and started saying all kinds of bad things about Kamal.

'I'm sure Kamal has not told you he's married.'

Monika looked at her, surprised.

'Oh, I can tell by the look on your face that he hasn't. Of course not. Well, he's married, he has two children.'

Monika was not sure how to react and Smelia, seeing the hesitation in her eyes, decided to go on.

'He pretends to be something he's not, Monika, like so many other men around here. They are all just trying to hook up with tourists like you.'

'I can't believe that, Kamal is always so nice.'

'That's exactly what I mean, he is two-faced, he beats his wife and leaves her alone in the house but he's nice and friendly to others. You don't think you're the first, do you? Everybody here knows what Kamal is like.'

Monika grew angry, not with Smelia but with Kamal. The poison had worked and the woman's lies had persuaded her to believe that Kamal's intentions were not good at all. Suddenly everything made sense to her: his apparent indifference at times, why they always met up in restaurants or on the beach, and why he would not always come home with her at night. She was kicking herself: how could she have fallen for this? How could she have been so blind? She did not wait for Kamal to return, but went back to the apartment and gathered her belongings. In her anger she had made up her mind to leave immediately and a little later, as she was standing outside the building waiting for the taxi she had called, Kamal saw her on his way back from dropping off the laundry.

'Monika, what are you doing here with your suitcases, haven't you taken them inside yet?'

'Go away, I don't want to see you anymore.'

Her reply did not make sense to him and neither did the anger in her eyes. Despite his insistence, however, she refused to explain herself.

'For God's sake, Monika, please tell me what is going on.'

Desperate now, he kept imploring her to explain. 'If you want to go, go, but please explain yourself to me.'

As the taxi was pulling up, she cried, 'You're an asshole, Kamal.

You're married and you have children. You never told me anything. You used me.'

'What are you talking about? I don't have a wife and children. It's nonsense, who told you that?'

Monika held her tongue, got into the taxi, gave him one last look and took off. Kamal was left dumbfounded.

He was determined to prove to his boss that he was a better person than she was. As soon as Monika had left, he went to the store and asked her what she had said to his lover. Smelia gestured she did not want to talk about it. He persisted, but she would not say anything about the matter. He later understood that Smelia had taken a shine to him and had cunningly driven him and Monika apart. He had noticed before that Smelia often asked him where he was going in his free time and that she would also turn up there, usually with friends. He thought no more of it, however. In his eyes, she was simply his boss and he had never had any other ideas or intentions. Now that he knew about it, he started to realise what she had been after all this time. Despite knowing about the dirty game she had played, he kept working at her store. He needed the money. More than that, however, he was mindful of his father's view of the world and wanted to demonstrate his moral superiority. He had entrusted a friend of his with the story and assured him that he had a better heart than she did. He wanted to believe that was true, although it was difficult for him to discern whether he was motivated by magnanimity or by his wounded pride.

The optimism that had filled him months earlier was gone and it took a great deal of willpower for him to get himself to the boulevard each morning to palm off as much as he could to passing tourists. Smelia was being particularly agreeable, hoping to restore their former relationship. One day she anxiously told Kamal that somebody had come by to tell her that the store, not much more than a wooden hut, would have to make way for a new building. The store was located on a rather dilapidated part of the boulevard. The beach was around the back of the store and it was surrounded by some small empty shacks as well as a disco in some run-down fire hazard of a building. There were plans to build a new hotel there. Smelia did not know what to do and Kamal eagerly took the opportunity to prove his worth. He asked around and soon found out that the owner of Hotel Slavija, a well-established hotel in the centre of Opatija, was planning to build a large new hotel by the beach. He knew the director by sight and decided to visit him. In the amiable way that had become his trademark, he told the director he was a souvenir salesman and that his livelihood was at risk because of the construction plans. Politely, but without appearing too meek and mild, he consistently addressed him as Mr Marko and asked him for a place where he could continue to work. He also suggested a possible location and to his surprise, the owner gave his consent, on condition that Kamal did business from a tent. The wooden hut had to go. Kamal also secured permission to use two storage units under the boulevard where he could lock away his wares and the tent at night. The following day he accompanied Mr Marko to the city hall for the necessary permits. Kamal was surprised how smoothly it all went. He was even asked to sign the application, even though the authorities did not normally value his signature. He suspected that Mr Marko's signature was in fact enough and that his was merely symbolic, but it nevertheless filled him with a sense of pride.

'We can keep the store,' he told Smelia when he came back with the impressive document from the city council with its signatures and stamps, holding it up to her face. She looked him in the eye then and realised he had done something she would never have been able to do. She looked embarrassed.

'Thank you, Kamal,' she said, elated. 'And Kamal...I'm sorry.'

For the first time, she had acknowledged what had happened. Kamal said nothing, but inside he was smiling.

∾

Kamal knew the man, Branko. He had known him since his first few months in Opatija. He was one of those guys who seemed to be everywhere and who was always poking his nose into everyone's business. Kamal had had coffee with him a couple of times and had been glad he had nothing to do with him when it came to business. Until now, that was, because Branko had just been appointed by the construction committee to oversee security at the building site for the new Hotel Admiral. One morning Kamal arrived at the storage units under the boulevard to unpack and set up the tent for the day's business. That same morning, Branko had apparently decided to start taking his new job seriously.

'Hey Kamal! You can't put all that stuff here,' Branko shouted at him from afar.

Kamal felt he was in a strong position with his permits, and he remained calm.

'Yes, I can. What do you have to do with it?'

Branko took a deep breath and squared his shoulders. 'I've been appointed inspector, Kamal, you have to get out of here with all your stuff.'

Kamal just smiled and continued setting up the stall.

'Pack up and get going,' Branko yelled, to no avail.

'What kind of a friend are you, Branko? Normally you and I drink coffee together and now this? And as a matter of fact, I have authorisation for this, I have a permit.' He saw the hesitation in Branko's eyes and started to enjoy the confrontation.

'Show me this permit of yours.'

'No, I can't just give it to you, Branko.'

The document was so valuable to Kamal, he was reluctant to take any risks. The argument escalated until Branko left, only to return with the police. Kamal showed them his permit. They were surprised. They were well aware of Kamal and his background and wondered how he had managed to get the documents. The signatures were real and the stamps were impressive. Branko slunk off and did not talk to Kamal for months.

Every day, Kamal erected the tent that served as their store and Smelia hung up the clothes and put the whole assortment of shawls, accessories and perfumes on display. Business was good that summer and Kamal earned enough to get himself through the coming winter. He did not see Monika again and as time passed, he rarely thought about her.

Kamal slid a stack of banknotes towards the Polish smuggler in exchange for a supply of amber and jewellery featuring semi-precious stones. He had a nose for shady business deals like these, which bordered on the illegal. They weren't exactly criminal activities, but there was a little more to it than just smuggling a few cartons of cigarettes or a couple of litres of liquor, which many people considered a sport rather than a crime.

As long as the citizens of the Eastern Bloc respected the borders of the Iron Curtain, they were allowed to travel. Many Poles, Russians and Czechs went to Yugoslavia. For them it was like going to America. Yugoslavia practised a form of communism unknown to countries in the Russian sphere of influence. People there had more opportunity, more freedom of movement, and suffered less oppression. Of course there would always be those who find a way to profit from such situations and so besides tourists there were also smugglers in Opatija selling their illegally imported goods.

They were predominantly Poles and Russians from the Baltic Sea regions who smuggled their abundant supply of amber to Yugoslavia. The wealthy tourists from the West who had an interest in the beautiful fossilised resin made for a profitable market.

The deal was his way of preparing for winter. That was the time when more elderly tourists came to Opatija, and they were keen to buy his amber rings, necklaces and earrings. Smelia witnessed his deals and knew he was planning to do some business. She saw him pay for the goods and take the stuff home. He hid the valuable haul in a deep closet.

The season was over. Smelia and Kamal had carefully packed their stock, cleaned the tarps, scrubbed the tables and stashed the whole lot in the storage units under the boulevard. They had agreed to work together again come spring. In spite of their personal difficulties, they were both aware that their partnership was a profitable one.

In his small apartment, Kamal had started to manufacture small items of jewellery with his amber. With his experience, it was not hard to imitate the rings and earrings he had bought and his stock grew quickly. He enjoyed practising his old craft again.

'Police, open up!'

He heard pounding at the door.

'What is it?' Kamal called, thinking there might be a fire or some other calamity, and he opened the door.

'We've come to check the premises,' one of the officers said. They came in and their attitude told Kamal they knew what they were looking for. They did not say anything and Kamal wondered if they would really take his insignificant smuggling that seriously. It seemed to him the police had more important matters to attend to. Searching the houses of every Yugoslav suspected of smuggling would be a full-time job. Eventually they found the package of amber and jewellery in the back of his closet, but he could tell from their comments that they were disappointed. It was not what they had expected to find. Altogether, they confiscated about five kilos of goods and he was told to come down to the police station the following morning.

Kamal did not just give up, however. That very day, he went to see a friend who was also a police officer. This friend, he knew, had done business with the same smugglers. He told him the whole story.

'You know I don't have any papers, you know my background. I need this to make money to get me through the winter. Can you help?'

His friend understood and went with him to see the commander next day.

'I gave him the amber to work with. He is skilled at making jewellery and we have a business agreement. It is actually my property and I would like it to be returned to him so he can keep doing his job.'

His friend was bluffing, but the commander believed him. Kamal got back his five kilos of contraband.

'So why were you at his place?' his friend casually asked.

'His boss, Smelia, reported a theft. Her storage units under the boulevard have been cleared out,' the commander answered. 'We didn't find any of the stolen goods at Kamal's place.'

Kamal lost it. 'Did Smelia actually mention my name in connection with the theft?'

He was already certain of the answer. The commander confirmed his suspicions.

'That witch! What a vile creature.' His friend said it and he thought it, and for the amiable Kamal this was one of the rare occasions in his life when he knew exactly what to do. This was the second time

Smelia had stabbed him in the back. Now he truly saw her for what she was, an evil woman feigning innocence, who had an endless number of dirty tricks up her sleeve. Much later, Kamal realised that some women will do anything to get what they want or to destroy what they begrudge others. He decided not to work for her anymore and never to see her again. Not long after, the case was solved. Workers who cleaned up the beach at night had a replica of the keys to the storage units and the police found the stolen goods at one of their homes.

Kamal was thirty-five years old now and for the first time in his life, he was standing in the city where his mother, Sadeta Adinovic, was born. He had not had the opportunity before, but now Kamal had taken the train from Rijeka to Sarajevo to search for traces of his family on his mother's side.

Previously, he had had neither the money nor the time, and after the painful experience with his family on his father's side in Travnik, he had also lacked the courage. He feared his search would be in vain. But it was the only chance he had to have his identity officially confirmed, and it was this realisation that finally convinced him to make the journey. He wandered through the city centre for a while and found a cheap guesthouse in a back street. In the days that followed, he looked for his mother's birth certificate in the municipal archives. His efforts were fruitless, however, and he proceeded to broaden the parameters of his search and even visited other archives in the area. Still he failed to find what he was looking for. He did, however, discover that his mother's brothers and sisters had died and that one of her sisters had married someone called Kenovic. The name rang a bell and he was certain he had heard his mother speak of this sister and her husband. After some research, he discovered his deceased aunt had had four children, one daughter and three sons. He had no trouble finding his cousin. Her name was Fikreta and she welcomed him warmly into her home when he suddenly turned up on her doorstep and introduced himself. He politely asked how she and her family were doing and whether she could tell him a little more about the other members of their family. The only thing he later remembered was that Fikreta had been proud of her youngest brother Ademir, who had gone to America to study film. Then he brought the conversation around to himself and why he had come. He wanted to know if he had indeed been born in Zagreb and where he was registered, so that he could obtain a copy of his birth certificate. Fikreta heard him out but replied that she did not know either, it had all happened so long ago. Kamal got the impression that she was avoiding his questions and did not quite understand why that might be. She proposed that she contact her eldest brother Mehmed, who might be able to help him. He left hoping that a meeting with his cousin from his mother's side would answer some of his questions, but also with the uneasy feeling that Fikreta had been keeping certain things from him. Kamal knew he could usually trust his instincts. The next day, Fikreta took him to her brother's office and left. Bosnian families are very hierarchical and it immediately became clear to Kamal that, as the eldest brother, Mehmed Kenovic was the boss. His appearance, his tone of voice and his office all indicated this was the case. They had a lengthy conversation in which Kamal described his life so far, making it clear to Mehmed how important it was for him to collect evidence that he had been born in Yugoslavia and use it to acquire proof of identity. As the conversation went on, Kamal realised his journey to Sarajevo had been a pointless one. Mehmed made it quite clear to him that he had no intention of exerting himself for a son of the Ustaše at a time when the socialist regime in Yugoslavia still regarded the fascists of World War II as enemies of the state, as traitors. He was afraid it would cast his law practice in a negative light.

'Mehmed, you could testify for me, to prove I was born in Zagreb.'

'I can't Kamal, how am I supposed to know about that?'

'You must remember me as a baby? You came to Zagreb with your father, during the war, when I was a baby.'

'No,' said Mehmed, 'that wasn't me.'

Kamal got angry and saw there was nothing to be gained from his cousin. 'You're lying, Mehmed, I know from my parents that you were with us a few months before we left Zagreb.'

Mehmed kept denying it and when Kamal got up, angry and about to walk out, his cousin said, 'Kamal, you cannot claim any rights, either.'

At the time, Kamal thought it an odd thing to say, but thinking it through later, he came to the conclusion Mehmed had said this because he feared that he, as Sadeta's only son and therefore her heir, would have the right to claim property that had possibly been left with others. He had not even thought that far ahead and it was not what he had come for. His mother's family thought he was after money, which was not the case. All he wanted was to have his identity confirmed, but again nobody was willing to help him.

He hated this country, the country his parents had been born in, where he too had been born, and he cursed Yugoslavia and his family, who were shutting him out.

Kamal came to the conclusion that there was nothing left for him here and he decided to risk another attempt at crossing the border into Italy. The place at Nova Gorica where he had been arrested before seemed worth another try, if only because he did not know of any other likely place. It was a long journey by train from Sarajevo, and one he could barely afford. He was not as naïve as he had been the first time. He booked a hotel room and observed the area around the station carefully for a number of days. It soon became clear to him that a lot had changed over the past few years. There were a lot more checkpoints and he saw frequent patrols along the most vulnerable points of the border. The Iron Curtain had been visibly strengthened and escape seemed virtually impossible. Having failed again, he returned to Opatija. He felt like he was destined never to escape this country, which had begun to feel like a prison. From that moment on he would always refer to it as 'Camp Yugoslavia'. It helped to consider his imprisonment as the result of outside forces conspiring against him. It kept the other thoughts at bay, those in which he blamed himself for travelling to Zagreb from Switzerland, those in which he could hear his father's words again, 'Kamal, don't ever go to Yugoslavia, there's nothing there for you and you'll never find anything there.'

1980 - 1985, OPATIJA

E very day he went through the same ritual, carrying his wares up to the boulevard from the little storage unit and devotedly draping the dark cloth over a low brick wall to show off his souvenirs to their best advantage. He always chose a place that would be in the shade, not only because he preferred this himself, but also because he knew that tourists would linger longer in the shade of the trees and would be more likely to buy something. The items he sold depended on the time of year. In spring the tourists were elderly couples who came to enjoy the early sun. He sold them the rings, necklaces and earrings inlaid with amber and the wood carvings carefully displayed on the black cloth. Summer was a time for families with young children. The little figurines made from shells that he had glued together in winter always caught the children's eyes. Seahorses, suns and fish made of shells with a mother-of-pearl sheen reflected the sunlight from the waters of Kvarner Bay. He also found there was a ready market all year round for small paintings, landscapes of the surrounding area he had painted himself in a naïve style, using oil paint on glass. And so Kamal became part of the display of worthless knick-knacks that stretched for hundreds of metres along the boulevard and into the cheerful-looking town of Opatija. He had decided he would no longer work for others, but rely on his own talents. Since then, he had been doing better business and although he had some bad days, he made a better monthly salary than he ever had with Smelia. He had, for now, come to terms with what he considered his fate. He would live from day to day and enjoy the oncoming summer. He always felt good by the sea. As he swam lazily in the Adriatic, the setting sun colouring the water red, he mused on the fact that water had always been his favourite element. In the evenings he would eat fish at a cafe by the water and when he took a day off, he spent it on the beach with his friends. They would look at women and search the beach with their eyes for any who were sunbathing alone. He and a friend would make bets about their chances of wooing them. Sometimes he would win, not just the bet, usually for a jug of wine, but also a couple of nights of sex and fun. It never meant anything more to him.

And then along she came: Doris Day. He saw her walking down the boulevard, a beautiful woman, a blonde with the same features and expressions as the film star from his youth. She was holding a small child by the hand and when she passed by his merchandise he instantly felt attracted to her.

'She's my type, always has been,' he told his friend. 'I used to go to the movies with my mother and I always liked Doris Day's films best. This afternoon I saw her again!'

Kamal, who was now thirty-seven years old, had seen the woman of his childhood dreams and every day he spent at the boulevard he kept his eyes peeled for her. It made him restless and at night he saw visions of her. Fragments of films came back to him and he felt nostalgic remembering how his mother would summon him to accompany her to the cinema where Doris Day would smile at him from the screen. Weeks passed and gradually his elation subsided. But then, one afternoon, as he was on his way to his apartment to fetch something, he saw her. She was entering the same apartment building. He thought back to the coincidence of Monika having rented a room in the same building and he wondered if history was repeating itself. He greeted her, and she returned the greeting.

'Are you living here?' he asked.

She replied that she had moved in a week ago. She had a room on the same floor as Kamal.

'Where are you from?' he wanted to know.

'From Rijeka.'

'That's only fourteen kilometres from here. What brings you here?'

'I don't want to say too much about it, if you don't mind. Family issues, let's leave it at that.'

Too bad for her, but good for me, Kamal thought immediately. He saw himself as her saviour. If he played his cards right, he might become involved, help her, give her advice. He knew the landlord was an unpleasant and aggressive man, especially towards women. Whoever came to live there, he was always out to sleep with and even forced himself on some women.

'Could you not find a better place than this? It's not good here for single women, the landlord is a nasty man.'

'Thank you for the warning, I already know, but I can fend for myself,' she answered with a smile.

A strong and beautiful woman, Kamal thought. He felt that it was safe to take the next step. 'Shall we go for a drink tonight to get to know each other better? Do you have time?'

'OK, neighbour,' she joked. 'By the way, what's your name?'

'Kamal. And you?'

'My name is Majda.'

Two syllables, just like Doris, Kamal thought.

Dusk fell and, at a bar by the sea, Kamal looked into the blue-grey eyes of Doris Day. The same beaming smile, the full cheeks, the medium-length blonde – albeit dyed – hair. Everything about Majda reminded him of the woman of his dreams. He could not keep his eyes off her. They talked about his life and hers. Majda Dodic was her name, born in Rijeka. Her parents were from a small village in what was now Slovenia, about thirty-five kilometres from Rijeka, and had moved to the harbour town in search of work. Her father had got a job as a mechanic at the big Third May Shipyard, named after the day Yugoslavia was liberated from the Germans. Her mother worked for a cooperative that produced wine. She had a younger brother who was training as a car mechanic at Rijeka Technical College. Majda told him she was a governess in Opatija. The child whose hand she had been holding on the boulevard was not hers. She did not speak of her family issue that first night. Kamal was mesmerised. Majda was beautiful, smart, and slim, and her smile was irresistible.

His 'saviour tactic' worked. He gained Majda's trust and she grew to like him. Her job as a governess was temporary and Kamal offered to look for work for her. He had many contacts on the boulevard and in the city centre. He knew everybody who had a store, restaurant or café and he soon found an old man who sold souvenirs who could do with some help. He sold wooden cups and other wooden items. Majda spoke a bit of English and Russian and, thanks to Kamal's mediation, the old man hired her and she soon became a good saleswoman.

In the evenings they often went out for drinks, mostly beer, because Majda preferred it to tea or coffee. They also went dancing. Majda was crazy about dancing. Kamal loved seeing her so happy and when he came home he was often humming 'My Dreams Are Getting Better All the Time', the Doris Day song he knew best. He imagined what it would be like to take her in his arms the following evening and kiss her in the moonlight like in the song.

A few days later, it happened. After a lovely night of dancing, they were strolling down the Lungomare. It was a beautiful boulevard, paved with natural stone, which stretched along Kvarner Bay for kilometres, all the way to Lovran. The moon was shining just as the song had promised and he had taken Majda's hand. He had been here before with other women and he had been more resolute with them, taking the risk of being rejected for granted. But now, with Majda, so much more was at stake. He felt insecure and did not want to force anything. She gently squeezed his hand and he took the gesture as the go-ahead to kiss her and when she returned the kiss, he said, barely audibly, 'My dreams are getting better all the time.'

One day, Majda introduced him to her mother, who had come down from Rijeka to visit her. She had not spoken to her 'little Majda' for a long time and she was in tears at their reunion. He listened to the conversation and, finally, the nature of the family issues that Majda had been vague about since their first meeting became clear to him. She had run away from home because her father wanted her to marry a man she despised, a brute without much of an education. Kamal was surprised that she had kept quiet about this for months. In his eyes, it was nothing new. In Lebanon he had heard lots of stories about arranged marriages that did not come about because daughters were no longer willing to comply with tradition, and stood up to their parents. Mother and daughter talked and drank wine and as the day progressed, Kamal noticed Majda's mother was getting drunk. Majda had a high alcohol tolerance, which Kamal attributed to the fact that she drank a lot.

The old man she worked for was a fervent drinker of white wine. He always had a bottle open in the store during the day and would ask Majda to have a glass with him. She easily drank three or four glasses of wine during the day. In the evenings, in Kamal's company, she switched to beer, and then often back to wine late at night.

'My mother often drinks more than she can handle,' Majda said after she left. 'It's her way of dealing with problems.'

'My father wants to speak with you', Majda said.

This came as a surprise to Kamal. It was a few months later and he had understood her father did not want to have anything to do with him. For a start, he was a Muslim, which was a sensitive issue in predominantly Catholic Slovenia. On top of this, Kamal was not Slovenian and, like many Slovenians, her father was very nationalistic. Mockingly, Kamal often said the only word Slovenians know is 'Nevem', which means something like 'I don't understand you'.

'If you speak to them in English, you might get an answer from them, but if you speak to them in any other language, the only reply you get is 'Nevem',' he explained. 'Slovenians only like other Slovenians, don't they? Your father didn't want anything to do with me and now suddenly he does?'

It turned out to be nothing but self-interest. Because of Majda's stories, Kamal had never been under the illusion that her father would ever make the effort to get to know his possible future son-in-law. Majda's father wanted to buy a car, a VW, at the factory in Sarajevo and he needed some German marks. Two types of currency were used in Yugoslavia. Daily necessities could be paid for in dinars, but luxury items were only available to those who could pay in dollars or, lately, in German marks. As a result, there was the official dinar exchange rate and a rate that was set on the black market. Dodic had saved up enough dinars to buy the car, but he did not know how to get hold of German marks. From Majda's stories, he had ascertained that Kamal knew his way round this business. Despite the antipathy he had started to feel towards the domestic tyrant, Kamal agreed to help him, hoping the relationship between Majda and her father might benefit. When the man arrived from Rijeka, he handed over a fat envelope full of dinars and Kamal set out to visit a dealer. He exchanged the money for marks. The regular commission was ten percent, half of which was for the dealer and the other half for the person who arranged the transaction. Kamal considered giving Majda's father the five percent, but decided to keep it for himself in the end, which turned out to be a good decision. He presented the envelope to her father, who pocketed it and left.

'Majda, what's going on? He's leaving without saying anything, he didn't even thank me!'

'That's just the way he is,' sighed Majda, who was used to a lot worse than this.

'Horrible man, I don't ever want to see him again,' Kamal said and he decided to ban her father from his life and from his thoughts.

~

The love between Kamal and Majda was passionate. He had never felt this attracted to any woman and they spent every possible moment in each other's company. They moved in together after a few months, both of them certain that their love would last for ever.

'Majda, will you marry me?' The question was often on his lips, but he did not ask her. He was confident of their love and not afraid of her answer. He knew she would say 'yes', but he was well aware that marriage was not an option, like everything of an official nature in his life, as he would need a passport. It bothered Kamal more than Majda. He valued traditions very highly, and felt strongly that his role as a man was to ask a woman for her hand in marriage. Perhaps he wanted it even more because it was not possible. He also valued marriage as a symbol of love and solidarity . Majda knew that his lack of papers was the reason they could not get married but their love was strong and she took it as a given.

'We will get married, Majda, when it becomes possible, as soon as we can.'

'That's good, Kamal, but you will have to ask me first,' she answered, laughing.

Kamal went down on one knee. 'Majda, dearest Majda, will you marry me?'

'Yes, Kamal, I will.' She had given her word and from that moment on they both felt like they were married, even though it would never be official.

∽

A long road wound its way up into the hills from the centre of Opatija. Recently, Kamal and Majda had begun walking up and down this road to work on the boulevard. They had found a small, brand new apartment a few kilometres away, in Pobri. The rent was reasonable, it was large enough for the both of them, nicely built and the view of the distant sea beyond the gentle hills was magnificent. All the signs were that a good chapter was about to start in Kamal's life.

He had not been able to open a bank account before, but now they had done so in Majda's name and he had deposited his savings in it. Every week they pooled their earnings and took what they did not need to the bank. Life was good and they were happy, until Majda became ill in the winter of 1981. She was pale and clammy, short of breath and complained of chest pains. Fluid in the lungs, the doctor said and he sent them to the hospital. Majda was diagnosed with acute pulmonary oedema caused by heart problems. It soon became clear she would have to be admitted for several days and because they were not insured and did not have a lot of money, Kamal was forced to go to her parents for help. He visited her mother at work in order to avoid her father and she promised to talk to her husband and see what they could do. The next day, her father visited the hospital and took care of the matter. Kamal did not know exactly what kind of deal he had made, he was just happy he had not encountered him and he heard later that the hospital bill had been paid in full. To him it felt like reparations, because in his opinion, Majda's father was in her debt. He also felt relieved that he had not been forced to break into their meagre savings. After twenty days, Majda was discharged from the hospital with a few boxes of pills in her bag to keep her heart rate regular.

Of course afterwards he regretted not keeping an eye on their financial affairs, but it had simply not crossed his mind and he trusted Majda. At the end of the week, he handed over his earnings and she took the money to the bank. Now and then he would ask her for money for extraordinary expenses and she would withdraw it and give it to him. On the first day of every month he would remind her to pay the rent and when he asked her about it at the end of the day, she would tell him she had taken it to the landlord.

'What are you doing? Is something broken?' Kamal asked one night when he came home from work and found the landlord kneeling by his door with a toolbox beside him.

'No, I'm changing the locks.'

'Why? I don't think there's anything wrong with them.'

'I'm changing all your locks.'

'But why, what's going on?'

'I'll show you what's going on.'

The landlord took Kamal to the little annex of the apartment building where Majda would hang their washing to dry when it was raining. They went inside and the landlord walked over to an old, unused cabinet and said, 'Look behind this cabinet.'

Kamal did as he was asked and saw it was full of empty liquor bottles.

'You can afford all that booze but you are three months behind on the rent.'

'How is that possible? I ask Majda to pay the rent every month and she does.'

'She doesn't, Kamal, I can tell you that.'

Only then did it start to dawn on Kamal.

'I'll give you one key and one week to find something else. After that, the place needs to be empty.'

Majda returned from the market with vegetables and bread.

'Why haven't you been paying the rent? We have money in our account, don't we?'

Majda did not reply and Kamal understood. 'There should be at least five thousand dinars in that account, maybe I can strike a deal with the landlord. Show me the bank statements.'

Majda appeared to be in shock, and did not respond. Kamal pulled open some drawers and found a folder hidden away in one of them.

'Zero! The balance is zero!' he exclaimed. The account was empty; Majda had withdrawn everything. 'And all those empty liquor bottles behind the cabinet, whose are those? Who drank all of those?'

Majda was sitting in a chair, her face pale and tear-stained. She did not know what to say. Suddenly everything started to fall into place for Kamal. Her preference for beer over coffee, her mother's drinking, the white wine she drank at work during the day.

'I thought you were the daughter of an alcoholic, but it turns out you're one yourself!' he yelled. 'Why, Majda, explain to me why?'

Majda remained silent. At best there would be some shallow excuse of an explanation that would not suffice. Her tendency to drink had deeper roots.

'We shall have to leave and find another place, Majda.'

They could see the stars between the roof tiles, and the windows were broken. Rain was uncommon on this part of the Adriatic coast and the few times it did rain, only a small amount of water came in. They had found the attic space through a friend after a lot of searching and asking around. They camped between the rafters for three months without water or electricity. After that, they squatted in an empty apartment for two months. Because of their circumstances, sales at the boulevard were going down. Majda had lost her job and life was hard and fraught with uncertainty. In the end, they found a place, a small, dark, ramshackle house. In that dismal little house, Majda found even more reasons to drink. She drank whatever she got her hands on at every opportunity and although Kamal kept imploring her not to, she persisted. Anger did not work, nor did trying to reason with her.

A doctor had recommended she get professional help, but they had no money to pay for it. Majda thought it would be of no use anyway. A plan began to take shape in Kamal's mind. He decided to take matters into his own hands and administer his own sort of therapy.

'You see where your drinking has got us. You're not going to stay at home any longer, you'll come to work with me and you'll stay with me all the time', he said in a commanding tone that Majda had not heard before.

'Why would I do that, Kamal?'

'Because otherwise I will leave you.'

She went with him to his spot at the boulevard, where she helped him sell his souvenirs. Every hour, Kamal took her to a café for a drink. He ordered a coffee for himself, and a glass of liquor for her. Not just a small glass, a double measure. Every hour, day in, day out, Majda drank and drank.

In the evenings, he brought half a litre for her and said, 'Do you want to die? If so I'll give you enough to kill you.'

It continued for a month before Majda said she had had enough. 'No, Kamal, please, I don't feel well.'

She complained of chest and stomach pains. The doctor diagnosed inflammation of the oesophagus and stomach lining and strictly forbade her to drink alcohol. He prescribed medication to help her stop drinking and for the crisis that would follow after she quit.

'Ah, none of that will help, anyway,' Kamal said when she returned from the doctor's. 'Just have a drink, I won't judge you. I'll have one with you.'

'No, I'd rather have tea.'

'I'll put in a splash of rum.'

'No! I only want tea. It's over, I don't want any more!'

This was what Kamal had been waiting for. Never before had he been so pleased to hear the word 'no'. This was the moment he had been hoping for, this was the course of therapy he had devised. It was untested, but it seemed to have worked for Majda. His euphoria was short-lived, however.

'Plus I'm pregnant Kemo, but I couldn't care less.'

Kamal could not understand. For a long time, Majda had kept it from him and now she had blurted it out. Majda did not think the child could have a future and her depression left her feeling indifferent. All he could do was focus on her 'no'.

'Now that you've had enough, that's enough for me.'

'What do you mean, Kamal?'

'Now that you're willing to quit, we can carry on together, but if you start drinking again, that will be the end of us.'

Majda said that she loved him and that she could not live without him. From that moment on, they moved forward together. Majda had the strength to stay away from alcohol, but the ominous feeling that she might fall off the wagon again stayed with Kamal for a long time.

They called him Kemo Junior. Majda and Kamal's first child was born at the hospital in Rijeka in 1983. Immediately after the birth, it became clear something was wrong with little Kemo. After a few days, he turned out to have a heart condition that would require surgery.

'But there are other complications,' the doctor had said, 'the baby is too small and has symptoms we have trouble explaining. I want you to answer me truthfully: did you drink a lot during your pregnancy?'

Majda could do nothing but nod her head. Kemo Junior turned out to have a severe syndrome, a condition caused by his mother's heavy drinking. Majda was forced to give up the child, and he was admitted to a home for children with physical and mental disabilities.

Kamal felt guilty about the therapy he had invented and pushed upon her and she felt guilty about her indifference. The guilt was even stronger than the grief.

~

Hindsight, Kamal was a man of hindsight. By now, he had been in Opatija for ten years and although, looking back, he would say life was good there, he also regretted not trying to build a life for himself in Sarajevo.

'I should have gone to the big city immediately,' he confided to Majda. 'Who am I here? A trader, a dealer, a junk salesman. I would have had a better chance of starting something there rather than here, with those stupid souvenirs.'

'But then we would never have met,' Majda responded.

He felt she could not understand his longing for a meaningful existence. He had never stopped yearning to cross the Italian border, never stopped yearning for a life outside Yugoslavia. The years he had spent there felt like lost time. People did not trust him, he was either regarded as a stranger without official papers, or as a son of the Ustaše who was not to be trusted, and should perhaps even be feared. He often felt ill-treated, even though he was friendly, paid his rent on time and stuck to the rules. His new landlord often made it clear that he was doing Kamal a favour by allowing him to live there without the proper papers. He needed a passport. It was a point he kept coming back to, he had to do whatever it took to get an official identity.

~

The huge grey eyebrows and sideburns were Lioubov's most

prominent features. Kamal had met the old gypsy in Opatija. They had chatted on several occasions when the man came to see Kamal on the boulevard. For a while now, Kamal had been selling tiger balm, a greasy ointment containing camphor and menthol. A lucrative business, since people used it to treat a whole range of ailments. The gypsy asked him where he bought the little jars of cream. Kamal vaguely said he had contacts in Zagreb.

'How much do you pay?' asked Lioubov.

Kamal thought that was none of his business and refused to be interrogated. The gypsy noticed his hesitation and asked him about the price again, adding that he was a trader too and assured him he could supply the balm for a better price. Kamal looked him straight in the eye.

'They cost me five dinars a piece.'

'Listen,' answered Lioubov, 'five dinars, that means you get a hundred for five hundred dinars. I can get you a thousand for two thousand dinars.'

Kamal took his time and recalculated twice. He had not lied about the purchase price and now Lioubov was offering them for two dinars a piece.

'That's a good offer, I'll take it.'

Some weeks later, Lioubov brought him a thousand jars of tiger balm from Bulgaria and he also brought a whole range of small bottles of perfume and jars of pomade.

'As a trial, you get these for free. See if you can sell them, then we'll talk about it.'

Kamal was satisfied, there was nothing wrong with the goods and Lioubov soon turned out to be a reliable business partner. The old Bulgarian lived in Belgrade and they met whenever he wanted to see the sea. It was the beginning of a friendship. Kamal did not know if the fact that Lioubov was about the same age as his father had anything to do with it, but the bond that grew between them sometimes reminded him of the way he used to talk with his father, their mundane conversations as well as the confidential ones. He felt at ease and he told Lioubov his life story. He revealed more to him than he had ever done before, telling him things he had not even told Majda. She knew that he felt like a prisoner in Yugoslavia and that he often felt ill-treated because people regarded him as an Arab or as the son of a war criminal. But he had never told anyone that he was embarrassed about who he was. He felt like a failure, like a man who could not be a real man, could not get married, did not have a bank account, had no rights, who had absolutely nothing. He confided his feeling of complete failure to Lioubov.

'All I have is a name, Lioubov, and sometimes people even doubt that, when it suits them.'

~

'The whole world hates us, we're cursed and we're ostracised. I know the feeling, Kamal,' Lioubov said. He was concerned for his friend. 'I have a plan, we can try to get you a passport through me.'

'What do you mean, through you?'

'We can set it up, we can say that I'm your father and that I'm looking for you. We can pretend I lost my son a long time ago, that I don't know where he is and that I'm searching for you now.'

'But how are you planning to do that?'

'I'll start by getting something in a newspaper,' Lioubov said. 'I'll get your story in the paper, and say I've lost you, with details that clearly only a father could know.'

Kamal accepted his proposition and although he doubted their chances of success, he was willing to do anything to acquire a passport. Damir Kunestra, a journalist for *Arena*, the local newspaper, was interested in Lioubov's story and wrote the article. Acquaintances of Kamal who read the story about a lost son failed to make the connection. Those few individuals who knew both Kamal and Lioubov and noticed how the specific details in the description of the lost son matched Kamal soon understood what they were doing. Kamal got the impression that they were sympathetic and would not betray him.

Kamal made the journey to Belgrade, with the article in his bag, to report to the local police station. He gave them the article to read and asked the officer if he knew the man who was looking for his son. It turned out that he did and soon more officers showed an interest in the case. There was no lack of sensationalism and before long Kamal was climbing into a police car. Another car with four police officers drove ahead of them in the direction of the neighbourhood where the old man lived.

After driving a few kilometres, the small police escort brought him to a door in the gypsy neighbourhood of Belgrade. An officer knocked on Lioubov's door.

'There's someone here who's looking for you', he announced. 'You wrote in the paper that you're looking for your son? Now here's someone who says he's your son!'

Lioubov let Kamal in and together they played out the scene according to their plan. Kamal was embraced, but meanwhile Lioubov gave voice to his feigned doubts.

'You've changed so much, Kamal, I barely recognise you.'

'Are you certain this is your son?' one of the officers asked.

'Not certain, but I think so. I'll know for sure if I see his feet, he has two fused toes on each foot.'

'Kamal, show me your feet.'

He took off his socks and shoes and showed his distinctive webbed toes. The officers looked on with curiosity. Any doubts had been dispelled and when Lioubov asked Kamal to show him a distinguishing birthmark on his shoulder, everybody was certain father and son had been reunited.

'My son, he's back!' Lioubov exclaimed, calling out through the open window, to a small crowd of neighbours that had formed outside, curious to know why the police were there. But Kamal and Lioubov's hopes were dashed when it turned out the police were unwilling to officially declare them father and son. Lioubov was asked for documents to verify his claim that he was Kamal's father. But there was nothing to register. They wanted proper evidence and fused toes did not count.

～

'Why don't you come and live with me?' Lioubov knew about the difficult relationship between Kamal and his landlord. 'I've got plenty of space. I could even register my place in your name.' Lioubov had moved to Grocka, a town on the right bank of the Danube, about thirty kilometres from Belgrade. There was an uninhabited little house on the plot of land he had purchased. 'Oh no, of course, that wouldn't be possible. We'll register it in your wife's name.'

'How much would that cost?' Kamal was interested in the offer because Majda was pregnant again and the security of having their own home suddenly felt very important.

'You can pay me five thousand dollars.'

It was a large sum, but it felt like a gift to Kamal. They wouldn't be able to get a house anywhere for that price. He cautiously explained the idea to Majda. He knew she would be reluctant to move. She still lived close to her place of birth and it felt familiar to her.

'We have the chance to get our own house, darling. It's true that it's far away and that things would change, but I really think we should do it.'

Majda agreed to take a look at the house first and they travelled to Grocka together. Although the place was small, to them it seemed magnificent. It had two bedrooms, a kitchen and a toilet. The matter was decided when Majda saw the smallest bedroom. With a baby on the way, she immediately started picturing how she would decorate the room. She agreed to the move and the house in Grocka was registered in her name. 'Majda Dodic', the deed stated, and she proudly signed. Kamal did wonder about Lioubov's motives for selling them the house so cheaply. He did not dare to ask him outright. Lioubov claimed it was because of their friendship, and although Kamal really wanted to believe this, he suspected it was not the only reason. He concluded that the old man just knew he was smart and worked hard and that he might profit from that. This later turned out to be true. In Lioubov's world, children were expected to take care of their parents as they grew old. He made it clear that he expected the same from Kamal.

'Kamal, you're my pension plan, he said.'

Lioubov could not let go of the fact that Kamal would be much better off with a passport. Together, they visited a lawyer with a good reputation and explained the situation to him.

'I'll let you know if there's anything I can do. I need a few days to do some research. We shall see.'

Three days later they visited him again, and the outcome of his investigations taught Kamal nothing he did not know already. He had heard it all before.

The lawyer spoke to Lioubov, completely ignoring Kamal. 'He has a Ustaše background, I don't want to get involved.'

Again, a door was slammed in Kamal's face. Every time he tried anything he failed and it seemed he was condemned to a life without official documents.

'I'm done with it, Lioubov.'

'What do you mean?'

'With trying to acquire these damned papers. I'm never going to succeed, I'm sick of trying.'

1985 - 1990, GROCKA

They were happy, although Kamal regretted the fact that his newborn son Adam would not have the name Kojadin. The boy was given his mother's name, Dodic. The initial feelings of happiness did not last long, however. After only a few months, Kamal started to notice how much things had changed and what it was like to combine two lives. His family and his home were not far from Belgrade but he still worked in Opatija. That was where the tourists were and selling souvenirs was still his biggest source of income. He travelled the six hundred kilometres home, taking the night train from Opatija at eight o'clock in the evening and arriving at Belgrade station at six o'clock in the morning. By half past seven, he would be in Grocka, where he would spend several days with his family before taking the same route back to the coast. In the first few weeks after Adam was born he made the journey as often as possible. It took a lot of time and money, however, and he made the trip less and less frequently, until he went home no more than once a month.

The responsibility of bringing in enough money weighed heavily on him. Sometimes he only managed to sell a few things and sometimes five or six days would pass without any sales at all. Now and then he was able to buy some necessities cheaply. He intended to send a package home every week, but he did not always manage to, and sending packages was costly. He had to take care of three people now, and then there were the train tickets, the packages. They were difficult times. On top of that, Majda became pregnant again the following year. Leo was born in 1987, and two years later, he became a father for the fourth time. Kamal did not manage to be there for the birth of his youngest son, Alan. He never wondered whether Majda was able to cope with taking care of three small children. He had enough on his mind.

It was not until nine days after the birth that Kamal returned from Opatija, just as Majda came home from the hospital.

'What's wrong, Majda?'

Kamal saw his wife trying to breastfeed Alan, but it was not going too well. Breastfeeding Adam and Leo had never been a problem.

'It hurts, Kamal, but I have no idea what is wrong.'

'I can see that, I think you should let a doctor take a look.'

Majda wanted to give it a few more days.

'I can't stay long, only three or four days. You should see the doctor now, while I'm here.'

In spite of his insistence, she did not want to go back to the hospital.

'It's already getting better, Kamal, you don't have to worry.'

Tourist season was still in full swing and it was even busier than in previous years. Kamal returned to Opatija in November and business was good.

She called at the end of January.

'You have to come home, Kamal. I'm ill, I can't bear it anymore.'

Never before had Majda been so clear about needing help and Kamal took the first train to Grocka. He found her lying in bed, weak and pale.

'Kamal, there's red fluid seeping out of my nipple. It's not blood, but it looks like it.'

'You're not a child, you're an adult. Why didn't you go to a doctor?' Kamal reacted angrily, but it was mainly out of concern. He contacted a doctor, who came to examine her.

'You have to go to a hospital for further examination as soon as possible.'

The doctor wrote a referral letter in Latin. They immediately took a taxi to the hospital in Belgrade, about thirty kilometres away, and checked in at the reception desk. They were directed to one of the pavilions and after some time they were received by a nurse with a large stack of papers in front of her. The first thing the nurse wrote down was Majda's name and a date that Kamal would never forget: 5 February 1990. The admission interview took a long time and in Kamal's eyes she had to answer thousands of questions about her life. She was asked if she had been ill before, if she had lost weight, if there were any conditions in her family, if she had been on medication before, how much she smoked or drank. Kamal could not see the point of the endless questioning, but he could not stay any longer. He had to get home to look after the children, whom they had put in day care.

'Are you this...? Are you that...? They drive you mad with their questions. Instead of just examining her, taking some blood and some x-rays.' Kamal was venting his frustration to Lioubov and they agreed to visit the hospital together the following day.

~

'I'm a friend of the family,' Lioubov said to the attending doctor. 'You can talk freely about the situation. Tell us, what is going on? What have you found? Does she need to stay?'

'We examined her yesterday and we took some x-rays.' The doctor turned to Kamal. 'Sir, I have bad news for you. Your wife has cancer.'

Kamal did not say anything. Of course he had known this could be the diagnosis, of course he had hoped it was something else, something harmless, and of course he had tried not to think about it, to ban all negative thoughts from his mind. The doctor continued, informing them that they were going to operate on Majda.

'Just a small procedure, to get a tissue sample for examination. We'll send it to Zagreb, where they will examine the sample under a microscope and the results will determine whether we proceed with surgery. It's possible that other measures will be necessary.'

Kamal understood that all was not lost, but the way the doctor had spoken to them made it clear that Majda might die. For a long time he had ignored that possibility. It seemed unreal and distant, but after their conversation, he could not put the thought out of his mind.

~

Every day, their neighbours minded the children and Kamal visited his wife. 'Inoperable' was the term the doctor had used when the results of the tissue analysis came back. The biopsy had shown highly aggressive cancer cells and amputating the breast would only exacerbate the risk of the cancer spreading through the rest of her body. Cytostatic drugs were the last resort, and soon an intravenous drip was inserted and bags with an violent-looking blue fluid were attached to the drip-feed.

'It's medicine, but it looks just like poison seeping in,' Kamal said to Lioubov, 'and it's not even certain it will help.'

The treatment lasted several weeks. Afterwards, all they could do was wait. Kamal continued to visit. Majda had lost a lot of weight due to the treatment, she was in pain and had no appetite. They kept their thoughts to themselves, though they both knew exactly what the other was thinking. They feared that the full truth might overwhelm them if they said it out loud and they both wanted to postpone that moment for as long as they could.

'I'm in so much pain, Kamal, such terrible pain, everywhere, I can't find any relief. I don't know what to do. I'm so tired.'

Kamal struggled to find the right words, and failed. He knew nothing would help or comfort her.

'I have to go in a bit, Majda, do something for work.'

It was a lie, but he could not stand to see her suffer so, did not know how to deal with her and with his own feelings of helplessness so he simply took off. He turned to Lioubov, the only person he could talk freely to.

'Do you think there's anything left to do, is there any way to save her? Is there any way to escape this misery, Lioubov?' It was his greatest wish and although he knew deep down there was no chance of recovery, he clung to the thought.

'We have to get her to a military hospital,' Lioubov suggested. 'They have better healthcare, they can do more for her there and have better medication.'

'And you could make that happen?'

'Yes, I think so, I know of a few ways.'

What these ways were exactly, what connections Lioubov used, Kamal never found out. But the following day, to his surprise, Majda was transported by ambulance to the Military Medical Academy in Belgrade, a famous hospital that was known to be one of the best in Yugoslavia.

Everything started all over again. The doctors looked at her status and at the results of the earlier analyses. Although Majda could hardly bear it anymore, they did all kinds of tests again. New analyses were performed, results were compared to earlier outcomes.

'The situation is grave, but we'll see what we can do,' the attending oncologist said to Kamal and Lioubov, who pretended to be his father during the hospital visits. Kamal felt restless and the next day he brought the children along at visiting hour, carrying the youngest in his arms. They had been asking questions about their mother for weeks and every time he had explained she was a little sick but that they could visit her soon. They were excited and soon they were running around the room. A nurse took them somewhere else to play.

'Why did you bring the children? It's not a good time, Kamal,' Majda remonstrated. 'I look so terrible and I'm so tired, I can't handle them right now.' But she was grateful to him. Little Alan, who was lying peacefully beside her, gave her comfort. She sensed Kamal had not just spontaneously brought the children without a reason, that he sensed what she had known for a long time.

'Everything will be all right, darling,' Kamal said without a trace of doubt in his voice. Meanwhile, every fibre of his being told him that nothing would ever be right again, that all his doubts were justified. When he left the hospital with their children, he was more keenly aware than ever that Majda would not live much longer.

A few days later, when Kamal and Lioubov were waiting at the train station to go to the hospital, he saw the mailman waving at him. He gestured to Kamal that he had a letter or a package for him. It turned out to be a telegram. Kamal tore it open and there it was: 'Your wife Majda Dodic died on 9 May 1990 at 4:30 hours.' Death did not need many words. Without saying anything, he gave the telegram to the old man. Kamal did not shed a tear. The shock was so great that he was unable to cry. Lioubov searched for words, because grief requires answers. But words failed him, so he ordered cognac for them. Kamal needed three glasses to calm down his inner turmoil before he was able to travel to the hospital in Belgrade one last time, to the love of his life, the mother of his children.

Majda was buried in Belgrade and when Kamal stood over her grave, he was reminded of his mother's grave in Bhamdoun and also of his father's in Lausanne. The people he had loved the most were spread over three cities, buried in places where none of them had been born and raised, where none of them belonged.

'What am I to do, Lioubov? I have three children. I have to work and take care of them. I don't know, I just don't know.'

Kamal was distraught and faced what seemed an impossible challenge. Several times he wished that he had been the one to die.

'It should have been the other way round. Majda could have taken care of the children and she had all the paperwork and the house.'

'Don't worry, we'll find a solution. I can take them.'

'What do you mean?'

'I could become their guardian. You can keep working and we'll find someone to take care of them when you're at work. That's what I'm thinking.'

It seemed like a feasible solution for this difficult situation and Kamal felt noticeably calmer.

~

'I have acknowledged all my children and my wife named me as the father every time she notified the authorities of a birth,' Kamal exclaimed.

'Your acknowledgement of your children is in no way legal. It's not just about identifying yourself as the father, but also about identifying yourself in the first place, which you are unable to do!'

Three days after Majda had been buried, social services made a house call. Two women in severe grey suits notified Kamal that they had come to pick up the children.

'What are you talking about? I'm making arrangements to get them good care. You don't have the right to take them.'

'Mr Kojadin,' the older of the two women said, 'you are the one without any rights. We know about the situation. You are not the lawful parent of these children, which unfortunately makes it necessary for us to place them elsewhere.'

'I could become their guardian and adopt the children, couldn't I? You know how these things work. I'm their father!'

'That may be, but officially it is not the case. Your wife had sole custody of the children. You don't get a say in the matter, Mr Kojadin.'

Her words hit him like a sledgehammer. He had three children and now it turned out there was nothing he could do for them. Thanks to the old gypsy's intervention, the social workers agreed that the children should be allowed to stay together and be placed in one foster home. As a result, the children were moved to a small town sixty kilometres from where Kamal lived. There were several families there who cared for orphans. They were paid by social services to raise them until they reached adulthood. After a month, Kamal went to see the children and get acquainted with the family they had been placed with. It was painful to see his duty towards his children being performed by other people, but in practical terms everything seemed to be in order. It was doubly painful to see that the foster parents were Serbs. God's punishment, that was what it felt like to see his children being brought up with ideas and religious beliefs so different from his own. Kamal could not think of a solution. He had no choice but to resign himself to what he called divine providence.

1991 - 1995, OPATIJA

Suddenly they came together, the big world of politics and Kamal's own small world. Majda was gone, he was able to visit his children only sporadically, and political tension was mounting in the region, bringing even more pressure to bear on his life.

Yugoslavia was a collection of several nations, brought together under one central federal government after the Second World War and held together by the great leader Tito. After his death and the fall of the Berlin Wall the mood in the country started to change. The nationalist sentiments of the different states that had always been there under the surface started to rear their ugly heads. Every politician in Yugoslavia knew that giving in to these feelings would bring about an explosion. They realised that breaking with Tito's policies would be the end of the Federal Republic of Yugoslavia, but there was no way to contain it.

In 1991 Franjo Tudjman, in his role as president of the state of Croatia, then still part of the Republic of Yugoslavia, declared Croatia independent. He was following the example set by Slovenia. Soon afterwards, in a surge of extreme nationalism, the flags and symbols of the Independent State of Croatia that had been mothballed years before were dusted off and put on display again. Prominent members of the Ustaše movement were rehabilitated. The Serbs reacted by establishing their own Serbian republic on Croatian territory, in the Krajina, where large numbers of Serbs lived. Serbs and Croats now stood face to face, as latent feelings of hate and decades of repressed revenge resurfaced.

Kamal noticed the increase in tension and aggression. All of a sudden, he was a son of the Ustaše again, even more so than before. In the eyes of many, he was a fascist and a threat to the Serbs. He no longer felt welcome and comfortable in the Belgrade area. It is a recurrent pattern all over the world: children being held responsible for the actions of their parents. They are believed to be no better than their father and mother. Kamal was the rotten apple that had not fallen far from the tree. During this new wave of ethnic hatred he was insulted and treated aggressively. He would never deny his father, though, even when he was being portrayed as a son of the Ustaše, the son of a traitor, a fascist, a criminal. He had never seen his father like that, quite the opposite. In his eyes he had had a serious, strict yet loving father.

There was not much he could do for his children and he was forced to accept that. He decided to go back to Opatija, the only place he knew where he felt safe. He was following in his parents' footsteps. They had often been forced to leave their home behind. From that moment on, he was no longer able to visit his children. He was scared to make the journey to Serbia in order to see his sons, especially because his name alone made it clear what and who he was: the son of a dirty Croat. He did not call them either. The war was in full swing by then and all parties set up checkpoints, controlling every form of traffic, people's movements and even the phone lines. Kamal was trying to keep his presence in Opatija a secret. As the war progressed, phone networks were destroyed and for many people it became impossible to stay in touch. And so Kamal lost all contact with his children and even with Lioubov.

Before he had left he had asked the old man to keep an eye on his three sons. 'Please Lioubov, visit them now and then and I beg of you, see that they have a religious upbringing, even though I know they will not grow up to be Muslims.'

'Why do you want that, Kamal?'

'Because I am against communism, I don't want them to become communists.' As he said it, he could hear his father talking. It was the same fear that he himself had grown up with. Lioubov was also a religious man and he understood.

It felt like a long time since Kamal had travelled to Opatija from Switzerland, hoping to find his family and build a new life for himself. In 1976 he had felt young and full of life, but now he had lost all of that energy. It felt like his life was over, pointless. He could not say what had changed exactly, but something in him had died. He stayed with friends, a few nights here and there, because he had no permanent home. He was always trying to make some money, but it was difficult, as the war had put an end to tourism.

'She might be a good match for you,' said the woman who owned the newspaper stand. She knew Kamal well and he helped her out sometimes. Kamal looked at the woman she had pointed out. He looked her over, frowned and shook his head almost imperceptibly.

'She's free, she's a widow, you should make contact with her.'

Kamal accepted her offer of an introduction. It was a calculated move. He did not find the woman attractive, but desperate times call for desperate measures. That was how he got to know Slavitza. His charming smile and gentle manner were his ticket into her life and her house. It was a marriage of convenience, although there was no actual marriage to speak of, nor did they have a physical relationship. Two people found each other in a time of war, not out of love, but for practical reasons. Slavitza had two children to raise, both with minor mental disabilities. Kamal needed a safe place and a roof over his head and, in return, he played the part of a father. To the outside world, they looked like a conventional family. Kamal went out to do odd jobs wherever he could and sometimes sell things. He brought home food, they cooked together and they took care of the children. There was not much more he could do. The few possessions he had were left behind at the little house in Grocka. He had been forced to leave his clothes, the furniture and all the materials and tools he had sent home over the years. He especially missed the tools he had collected, because he thought there might be opportunities to work as a frame maker in Opatija. Slavitza received a meagre widow's pension and, with Kamal's irregular additional income, it gave them just enough to live on. Kamal still had some savings, and as the war continued, he was forced to draw on these reserves. He and Slavitza had an understanding; a relationship based on mutual sympathy and shared interests.

Kamal's life was all about survival. The days passed in a dull daze. He felt like he was no longer participating in real life and was out of touch with his own feelings. Almost mechanically he got up in the morning, performed his duties, chewed his food and smoked his cigarettes. Only at night did he feel a little more alive. Almost every night he woke up with tears in his eyes. Majda visited him in the small hours, brought him to life and made him feel the pain of human existence. The emptiness she had left behind was even larger than the space she had filled when she had been alive. On those nights, his mind played a miserable, unstoppable game of 'if' and 'then'; if Majda had not died, if his boys had not been taken from him, if that bloody war had not happened, then yes, then his life would have been so very different.

The progress of the war was unpredictable. Tensions between Croatia and Bosnia were mounting. People now clashed more often on grounds of national origin and religion. Muslims and Catholic Croats who lived in Bosnia now opposed each other. This affected the political climate in Croatia, where differences between Muslims and Catholics had not caused too many problems before. The politics of the country were now such that Muslims were no longer equals but a minority in a country dominated by Croats. While in Serbia Kamal was regarded as a Croatian fascist who did not belong there, in Croatia he was mostly seen as a Muslim. Kamal cursed this pointless war in which he did not feel like he belonged to either side. In uniform they all looked alike, Serbs, Croats and Bosnians. He felt the growing pressure on Muslims, was aware that the general mood in Opatija was against him, and he started searching for a way out, without telling Slavitza too much about it.

At the end of 1995, the Dayton Agreement brought the civil war to an end. His father's ideal, an independent Croatia, became a reality, although the country was considerably smaller than the Greater Croatia his father had envisaged. To Kamal it just meant greater restrictions, for Yugoslavia was now completely divided and new borders had formed. A period of reconstruction seemed to lie ahead and Kamal had decided the same should apply to his life. He was now in his fifties, longed for a new future, a new life, and he could not shake off the feeling that it was now or never.

'Hassan, how are you? Are you in Zenica?'

'Yes, Kamal, I am. It's good to hear from you.'

Finally, finally Kamal had managed to get in touch with his good friend Hassan. He had often tried to contact him in the last few years. Phone lines were not working properly and phone numbers and addresses were often outdated. He had heard on the grapevine that Hassan was staying in Zenica, a city in central Bosnia, and in December 1995 they got back in touch.

His friendship with Hassan had begun in the early eighties, around the time he had fallen in love with Majda. He was an Iraqi who had fled the war between Iraq and Iran and was studying at the Faculty of Tourism in Opatija. Kamal met him in a bar where Hassan had been speaking loudly in Arabic. Kamal made it clear he spoke the language too, which was uncommon for a Yugoslavian. That is how they met, and a friendship soon developed between the two men.

Kamal brought him up to speed about Majda's passing away, having to give up his children and his life during the war. Hassan was working in Bosnia for a humanitarian organization from the United Arab Emirates. Quite a number of Arab countries, the Emirates among them, were assisting the Muslims in Bosnia, who had flocked there as a result of the war.

'I'm looking for work and I want to get out of here. Is there anything you can do for me, Hassan?'

'I'll try. I'll call you if I hear of anything.'

And with that, the conversation ended.

Kamal could not help himself from playing the 'fate' card when he was trying to make sense of his life. It was not just coincidence or bad luck, but fate that had brought him to Yugoslavia and made him lose Majda. It was destiny that his children were being raised by Serbs and now he placed his future in Hassan's hands, assuming fate would run its course. Seven months later, in July 1996, Hassan called.

'Kamal, do you still want to come here?'

'Yes, of course. What took you so long, why did you make me wait?'

Hassan was silent for a moment. Kamal's answer had sprung from his despair and he feared his bluntness had startled Hassan.

'I didn't forget about you, Kamal. I needed some time, but I can help you now. Go to Rijeka train station tomorrow. A jeep with diplomatic plates will be waiting there for you. The driver is a doctor, he will bring you.'

'Bring me where, Hassan?'

'Bring you here, to Bihac, where I am now. I have a job for you.'

He did not tell Slavitza much, only that he was going to Bosnia to find work. Again, he left most of his possessions behind and took only a travel bag full of clothes to the station the following morning. He was thinking about his father, about the moment he had left Croatia. It seemed like history was about to repeat itself. It was like he was outperforming his father when it came to leaving behind everything he had built up. The SUV with the diplomatic plates arrived according to plan.

1996 - 2007, BIHAC

The jeep was approaching the border between Croatia and Bosnia. Kamal sat next to the driver, feeling uncomfortable. He had had too many bad experiences trying to cross borders and was already imagining how this adventure might go wrong. The doctor handed over his passport and medical card to the border guard and reported that he was on his way to the hospital in Sarajevo where he worked. He did not mention who his passenger was. Kamal did not know for sure whether they thought he was a patient who was being transported, or if the diplomatic plates decided the matter. In any case, Kamal was allowed to cross the border with surprising ease, without any interrogation.

He arrived in Bihac and there he met Hassan, the always cheerful and welcoming friend who reminded Kamal of the best period of his life, the years he had spent as a young man in the vibrant city of Beirut, surrounded by his Arabic-speaking friends.

'I'm happy you're here, Kamal. You can help me with all the things I have to do.'

The humanitarian organization from the United Arab Emirates

that Hassan was working for offered aid to the Muslim population in Bosnia, so it was very useful to him that Kamal knew the language and ways of the Balkans, as well as spoke Arabic. He also felt that he could trust Kamal. The work of these humanitarian organizations was vulnerable to abuse and fraud. Hassan was certain Kamal could prevent him from being conned by hustlers, fakers and other shady types.

Many Bosnian inhabitants of Bihac and the surrounding area, especially women whose husbands had died or disappeared during the war, came to them for help. They usually provided them with goods like flour, other non-perishable foodstuffs and firewood to get them through the winter. Kamal's job was to register those who applied for help and to document what goods they received. Alongside his administrative duties, he would also ask in-depth questions about the urgency of the help they requested, usually trusting his own intuition. Sometimes he pointed out cases he was not certain about to Hassan and together they would investigate whether the application should be denied or not.

It had been a long time, but Kamal had a proper job again. He was paid a monthly salary of four hundred markas, which was more than he had earned for years, and he also received shelter, food and clothes. The organization operated out of a local warehouse with half a dozen rooms. Most of it was used for storing goods but one room was set up as an office and Hassan lived and slept in another. At first, the two men shared the space. Hassan apologetically explained that it was a temporary arrangement and that he was looking for a better place to live. Kamal was satisfied with the accommodation and with the work he did. He mattered again. A few months later they found suitable housing in Bihac, at some distance from the warehouse, which meant their lives would no longer be all about the job.

Kamal finally got the chance to think about other things and it became clear that his language skills were proving handy again. There were several other humanitarian organizations operating in the area, as well as military units from Italy, France, Britain and several Arab countries as well as bodies like UNHCR, the UN refugee agency. He decided to look for a job as an interpreter alongside his work for Hassan. The standards were high and he had to take some exams. He passed both the written and oral tests. After the lengthy procedure, they promised to call him. He waited for days. When no call came, he went back for an explanation.

'You are not presentable enough,' one of the personnel officers who was involved in the selection procedure said.

He knew his appearance had known better days. Because of the war he had lost a lot of weight and a couple of teeth. But still, he spoke six languages. Nevertheless, he was not considered eligible for the job. His competitors were called Leila, Amira and Marija. Beautiful young women whose language skills were not as good as Kamal's, except for their body language.

'Yes, well, Kamal, that's discrimination for you. In Belgrade you're a fascist Croat, in Croatia you're a dirty Muslim and here you're just a filthy old man,' Hassan joked, summarising the tragedy of Kamal's last few years in a single sentence.

The blood ran down his hand and trousers, yet Kamal was oblivious. He was looking for his finger in the pile of wood shavings and logs around him. A little later he carried the sawdust-coated finger to a doctor in a little plastic bag.

'I think it will be no use stitching it back on.' The doctor judged the procedure unlikely to be successful. 'I think you will get used to it in three or four months.'

'You're the doctor, you know what's best,' Kamal replied.

'It's better to leave it', the doctor decided.

In hindsight, Kamal regretted being so obliging. Distributing wood had been one of his duties. A hundred cubic metres of wood would be delivered on a regular basis and given to those who needed it for the winter. Some received one or two cubic metres, some got three, depending on the family situation. One day, a woman asked him for some wood, as she had a large family. Kamal knew of her situation and he pitied her, so he promised her three cubic metres. He even added that she should also try other organizations. Kuwait, Libya and Iran also offered help in Bihac. He winked and said, 'If you ask them for help, don't tell them we've already given you three. Maybe that way you can get more.'

He walked over to the wood pile to set some wood aside for her when she asked him to split the logs for her. They had a splitting machine available for general use. The woman was scared to use it herself, though. It all happened in a moment. Some sawdust had flown into his eye just as a knot made the log split in an unexpected way. It was not even the saw blade but a sharp section of wood that cut off his finger, leaving him with a lifelong memento.

It was clear to Hassan and Kamal that their line of work would come to an end at some point. If they wanted to keep their jobs, they would have to find new ways of offering aid to citizens in the stricken areas that would also be beneficial to themselves. Hassan came up with the idea of drawing up plans for repairing and rebuilding damaged or destroyed houses, mosques and churches. The local manager of the organization gave them the green light and the funds to perform an inventory. This new task would fall mainly to Kamal. He had all the names and addresses of the residents of Bihac and the surrounding area who had come to them for help. Now he visited all these people to take a look at their properties. He discovered that many people lived in houses that were not theirs. They were mostly houses that had been abandoned during the ethnic cleansing and were now inhabited by people whose own homes had been destroyed. Kamal asked the residents to show him their damaged or destroyed homes, and was thus able to make an accurate assessment of the situation. It was a time-consuming task and Kamal did not hurry. He was guaranteed a monthly income and the work was not too taxing. He had a driver who took him to all the locations and he took his time talking with the residents, who greatly appreciated it. He drank tea with them and made notes on everything he saw. He had a computer file in which he processed all the information, gradually compiling a thorough overview of the housing problems in Bihac and the surrounding area. There were more than sixty houses that had been completely destroyed and were in desperate need of repair. The next thing he did was to map the damage that had been done to mosques and churches. He expected that the United Arab Emirates would be especially keen to rebuild the mosques and that there was a big chance they would obtain the necessary funds. He surveyed twenty places of worship altogether, some of which were so damaged that they would need to be completely rebuilt.

For two years he worked on the plans before Hassan submitted them, and by that time Kamal had already come up with a new project. Many rural residents of the countryside around Bihac had lost their livestock during the war and wanted to revive the smallholdings that had always been important to the local economy. Kamal got started on a new inventory, driven in part by self-interest. He recorded the demand for cows and sheep in the area. He also came across people who wanted to farm chickens or keep goats, and he worked out a programme for this too.

'Three percent, Hassan, do the maths,' he said. 'For every delivery we receive three percent, that could be pretty good money.'

Kamal felt like a smart businessman again, as he had been in Lebanon, where he had occasionally made such lucrative deals. He made a deal with some livestock merchants. If the programme came through, he would get commission on every delivery. Finally he was able to do something that Hassan would profit from as well, to thank him for all the help he had given him.

~

Fahira was young and beautiful and Kamal was surprised she was interested in him. He was not as thin as he had been and he had had his teeth fixed, but this woman seemed to be way out of his league. When he was distributing relief supplies, there were plenty of women who tried to befriend him, mostly just for the advantage of having a man around the house. He had never responded. But there was a click with Fahira. She made jokes that made Kamal smile that charming smile of his. More and more often she lingered in the warehouse, brought biscuits and drank tea with him.

'And what about women, Kamal?' she asked. 'Do you have many, or just one special one?'

He hesitated. 'One special one', he answered. 'There was one', he added. 'One who broke my heart into little pieces.' He told her about Majda.

Their love gradually grew, unimpeded by the thought of Majda. One day, they concluded that they were in a relationship. It felt good to realise he could still feel the way he did all those years ago when he saw Majda on the boulevard in Opatija.

He wondered what it would be like to marry a Bosnian woman. He did love her, it would not just be a calculated move, but it would still be a chance to get his life back in order. There were some complications, however. Her family were against him. Although he was a Muslim, like them, Fahira had told them he was Lebanese, to hide his Croatian background. That was still enough for him to be regarded as an outsider and that displeased them. On top of that, her sister became quite jealous. Single men were scarce, and now that Fahira had landed one, her sister became even more aware that she had not. Her mother opposed the relationship too, because Kamal was almost twenty years older than her daughter. But Fahira did not give in.

'Whether you approve or not, I will do whatever I want,' she cried and not long afterwards she moved in with Kamal, in the apartment he shared with Hassan.

Suddenly, it was all over. Two men had come over from Dubai to investigate. Fraud, apparently, and Kamal and Hassan were both interrogated. The authorities of the United Arab Emirates had been tipped off by an employee of the relief organization from Saudi Arabia that was located in the warehouse next door. The employee had seen a group of people he did not know at the Emirates' warehouse one Sunday. They were accompanied by the local manager of the organization. A truck was loaded with goods and left. It seemed suspicious and the employee had started to observe the warehouse after working hours. The pattern soon became clear to him: a truck was frequently loaded with goods before driving off in the direction of Travnik. The local manager, whom everybody trusted, seemed to be at the centre of the fraud. Kamal and Hassan were not charged but the price they paid was high. The warehouse was closed and the flow of funds was cut off. It was early 2000. Kamal was back at square one.

The lucrative dream of the three percent was not to be and Kamal had to come up with a new way of making money.

It soon became clear that the rules in the new state of Bosnia-

Herzegovina did not offer any new prospects. He had no chance of a normal job because he did not have any papers. He could not get permission to open a store and Fahira's intentions of marrying him also went awry due to his lack of official documents.

With the money he had saved up over the last couple of years, he tried to fall back on what he knew, and started his umpteenth small business. This time, he tried selling clothes on Bihac market. He purchased garments manufactured in China and just about managed to sell them at minimum profit in the aftermath of the war, when nobody had any money to spare. In a desperate attempt to turn the tide he tried to expand his range of goods with coffee and tea, but it hardly made any difference.

He did manage for a while, but then Hassan left in early 2002, first for Croatia and then on to Belgium. The precarious balance of his life became very clear. The rent for the apartment was now his sole responsibility and by the end of the year he had burnt through all of his financial reserves. Fahira had been forced to return to her family under threat of being disinherited and the owner of the building came to terminate the contract because of overdue payments. Kamal was back on the streets.

'Would you mind working as a shepherd?'

Kamal had been spreading the word that he was looking for work and someone he vaguely knew from the market in Bihac suggested it. 'I don't mind, as long as I have work', Kamal answered, desperately.

The man knew someone who had three hundred sheep and was looking for somebody to take care of the flock. The deal was quickly done. Kamal was willing to do anything and a salary of three hundred markas, a daily meal and some cigarettes was at least something to live on. He was given a place to sleep in an old caravan in the field and he had to learn to work with six dogs to guard the flock. He stayed with the flock in the fields for the entire season, from April until the end of September, returning to his ramshackle abode every evening. He had covered the caravan with a piece of orange tarpaulin and tied it down with ropes to prevent the rain from dripping in. That was all there was, and when night slowly fell in the hills, Kamal hoped the moon would light his unlit den.

In the beginning, or at least in the first year, he still told himself that he was Kamal Kojadin, that there would be more opportunities, that he spoke six languages, that he had mastered a trade and that he was a good salesman. At night he looked at the sky and pondered his fate, believing everything was written in the stars. Not in the way that lovers feel they are destined to be together, but the way disasters and disease scourge humanity. To Kamal it all seemed like a big game played by God and he wondered if God still believed in him. Later, his mind went quiet. The stream of thoughts stopped. He still talked to the dogs, but no longer about himself. The weather and the sheep were the only topics and as long as he talked to the dogs, there was no space for other, bigger thoughts and emotions. Days passed without so much as a glance at the sky. His back bent, he would cross the slopes where the sheep wandered. He sometimes felt like he was wandering too, and this thought often overpowered him and filled him with regret. Only the dogs reminded him of his task and made him look up now and then.

In winter he lived in a tiny room under the roof of a farm building. Every day, he let the sheep out into a field that he had fenced off. Then he would go into the stables to shovel piles of manure into a wheelbarrow and empty it on the dung heap. The sheep would stand motionless on the snowy hill, waiting until they were allowed back to the warm stable and their food.

The winter was so depressing that he actually looked forward to spring and his lonely existence in the fields. There, he lived with the dogs and built an enclosure from the metal grills normally used for reinforcing concrete. He weaved branches through the framework so the sheep had a place for the night. He had a gun to protect himself. Sometimes the dogs would start barking in the night and he would light a fire to keep away the wolves, wild boar, and even the occasional bear.

Kamal was alone and his mind was mostly empty. He had lost all sense of time. Only the weekly visits by the owner, who brought food for him and the dogs, reminded him of the days of the week and the passing of time. And so he passed the years in the hills around Bihac. It felt as if he were waiting, though he did not know what for. He barely existed as an individual, he was tough as leather, an animal amongst animals. He sometimes still had hope things would turn around, that there would be a sudden change for the better, although he had no idea where it would come from. It was a paltry sort of hope, as wretched as the life he was living.

A police car approached the farm. Kamal was busy cleaning the stables and saw the car coming. The farmer's wife was home and she spoke to the officers.

'Does someone called Kemo work here?'

'Yes, he's working over there.'

The officers came over to him.

'Are you Kemo?'

'Yes, that's what my friends call me. My name is Kamal.'

'Do you know a man called Hassan?'

Kamal confirmed this too, and the officers asked him if he knew where Hassan was.

'Why do you want to know, what has he done?'

'He's not done anything, but we are looking for him.'

Kamal was suspicious and, although he knew Hassan had gone to Belgium, he told the officers that he believed his friend had moved to Split to work at the reception of some hotel. The officers were not in any hurry to leave and in the conversation that followed it became clear to Kamal why they were looking for Hassan. He had been working in Bosnia since 1994 and every year, his work visa had been extended. Under Bosnian legislation, people had the right to apply for Bosnian nationality after seven years. That was the reason they had been looking for him. Kamal was surprised and inwardly resentful. An Iraqi who had been working there for seven years had more rights than he did, a man who had been born in the Balkans and whose father was from Bosnia.

Kamal had returned to his work when the police car drove up to the farm again.

'We were thinking, Kemo, we don't actually know you. What exactly is your name?'

'Kamal Kojadin,' he answered, feeling caught and cornered. He had entered Bosnia illegally and in all those years he had never had any dealings with the police, contrary to his experiences in Opatija.

'Do you have an ID card?'

'No, I don't, I have a travel pass, a laissez-passer. I emigrated to Lebanon years ago and came back to Yugoslavia and now I work here.'

He fiddled with the facts a little and hoped his answer would pass muster.

'Could you show us your travel pass?'

'Yes, of course, but it's no longer valid, I neglected to get it extended' was his next lie.

'No problem, show us anyway.'

Kamal went to his sleeping quarters to retrieve the heavily thumbed document and showed it to the officers.

'Listen, Kemo, you have to come see us at the station. We want to know a bit more about your life and about how you got here. We want to know how it's possible that you are here without papers.'

They left after telling the farmer's wife they expected to see Kamal at the station at ten o'clock the following morning. That evening, Kamal put all his cards on the table with the farmer. For all those years, they had never spoken about his identity. Kamal told him about his background as the son of an Ustaše supporter and about the problems this had caused. His employer had previously shown himself to be a blunt and unpleasant man and this was the first time any kind of understanding developed between the two men. The farmer's father had served in a division of the German SS during the war. He was even willing to take Kamal to the police station the following day. He was received pleasantly enough, was given coffee and was questioned in a friendly manner. Everything he told them was noted down. As a result, the police in Bihac had compiled a six-page dossier on Kamal before they let him go.

A few weeks later, Kamal was summoned to the station again. This time they wanted fingerprints. It turned out they had done some serious work on the Kamal Kojadin case. Officers had contacted Interpol in Lebanon and had received confirmation from Beirut, with copies of his Lebanese refugee identity card and his fingerprints as proof. Everything they knew about Kamal and his parents had been added to his file. Fingerprints were compared and found to be a match. The police were no longer suspicious and they even promised Kamal they would send his details to the Centre for Aliens in Sarajevo to see if he could get an ID card based on the material they had gathered. He knew what to expect. Although his story was valid, his fingerprints matched and they had Interpol's confirmation, there was nothing anyone could do. The authorities denied the request.

The feeling of solidarity between Kamal and his boss was short-lived. It was not long before he stopped receiving his monthly salary. Kamal did not know if this had anything to do with his boss's awareness that he was employing a citizen with no rights. The man said he was short of money and could not possibly pay him. Although Kamal did not believe a word of it, he felt forced to stay. He was dependent on him, and he was also sick. He had a stomach ulcer and felt weak and exhausted. The man was hard on him, malicious even. Kamal realised that the dog that always followed the man around got more respect than he did. He felt like an outcast, a pariah. He withdrew into the caravan, neglected the sheep and wallowed in his misery. He thought about his children, whom he had not seen for years. He calculated their ages and tried to imagine what they would look like now. Maybe one of them was sick, or even dead. He knew absolutely nothing about them. He was alone, homeless and cut off from the world.

One day he started vomiting blood. The farmer did not care to have a sick farmhand, and so he dropped him off at a bus stop without any money. The bus driver immediately saw Kamal was in a bad way and let him get on, even though he could not buy a ticket. At the station in Bihac, the driver gave five markas to a taxi driver to get him to the hospital. He had a bleeding ulcer, a life-threatening condition and the emergency department was obliged to take him in, despite his lack of papers and health insurance. He was rushed to an operating theatre. In a risky operation, he had part of his stomach removed. Afterwards, he stayed in the hospital for over two weeks. A social worker came by to check why he was not insured. Kamal explained his situation and social services were willing to pay the hospital bill. That was all they could do for him and Kamal received fifty markas to get back to where he came from.

Kamal went to the centre of Bihac and found temporary shelter with an acquaintance. Once more, he began to search for work. Kamal knew a man who grew and sold mushrooms.

'Give me twenty tubs each day,' he said. 'In the evenings I will bring you the money and you can give me half a marka for each tub I have sold.'

The man agreed and Kamal usually managed to sell the mushrooms so that by the end of the day he had earned ten markas.

'Kamal, my husband wants you to come by, he has a popcorn machine for you.'

The wife of the sheep farmer had suddenly turned up at the place where he was staying. The farmer had promised him before that in wintertime, when the sheep were stabled, he could use the machine. Kamal knew he had two of them, but so far it had been nothing more than a vague promise. Kamal knew that selling popcorn in the streets was a good business, so the offer appealed to him. He overcame his reluctance and again made the journey to the sheep farm outside Bihac.

'Could you mind the sheep for a few more days, Kamal? The machine needs a few small repairs.'

Kamal agreed, but the repairs were postponed. Kamal realised he had been lied to, but he stayed nevertheless, just because he had no other prospects. He excused his behaviour by thinking about his mother who had told him everyone has a good and a bad side and that he should accept both.

Again, he traversed the hills that prompted such sombre thoughts. Again, he sat in the dark, dank caravan, until the moment came when he just switched off, the moment he stopped existing. The view of the hills around Bihac by day and the light of a fire and the moon by night was all he had. No future, no expectations.

Until early 2008 he worked as a shepherd for nothing but board and lodging, although this was too grand a word for the caravan. He was being exploited by a profiteer with no conscience who had realised he was dealing with a man who had no way out. Kamal became ill again, although it was unclear what exactly the matter was this time. The farmer realised Kamal was in a bad way and was keen to get rid of him before he could give him any trouble. Again, he dropped him off at a bus stop, on the way to Sarajevo this time, handed him forty markas and abandoned him. Thus, Kamal arrived in the city a few hours later. He had managed to stay upright for as long as he could, but now he stumbled and hit the ground. Years of poverty and loneliness had taken their toll, he felt them in his weakened body, he saw them in his face, and his mind was dominated by a single thought: there is no promised land.

2008 - 2012, SARAJEVO

Kamal had found a place to sleep not far from the Sacred Heart Cathedral in the centre of Sarajevo, and had made a bed out of cardboard boxes. The large, old, yellow building had been partially destroyed by a fire and had been deserted for years. It was not hard to break in. He found a few boxes under some stairs on the first floor and used them to cover himself up at night. He used the last of his money to buy some bread and cheese every day. He begged for cigarettes to make his markas last as long as he could. He coped for two more weeks before he had to start begging for food as well. The homeless and beggars had always seemed to be part of another world, but now it was one he belonged to himself. By the large fountain, not far from an ATM, he found a place to sit. He felt desperate as he started to ask people who had just withdrawn cash for money.

'One marka, half a marka?'

Most people did not give anything. Kamal had a beard, his face was tawny and he looked very weary. Everything life could demand from a man it had demanded from him. A man looked him in the eye and gave him five markas. That would keep him going for a while.

The popcorn vendor he had met on the streets offered him a place to sleep. His name was Nermin and Kamal stayed at his house for a couple of nights. He put Kamal in touch with a tradesman who sold souvenirs at the souk in Sarajevo. The man had been robbed shortly before. Burglars had broken into his small wooden kiosk at the market and taken most of his wares. The man asked Kamal to be a night guard. He got a mattress and a blanket and, for a salary of five markas a day, he slept among the copper pitchers and vases. That much hardship can blur the line between right and wrong. His nightly presence among all the stalls of food and goods made it very tempting to commit some petty theft to make his life a little easier. Yet it never occurred to Kamal to violate the merchant's confidence. For two months he did the job and he was quite happy with it. He had a bed, a dry place to sleep, a bit of money to buy food and sometimes the owner of the kiosk would unexpectedly bring him something to eat. But his days were empty, he had no plans to speak of and so he roamed the Baščaršija, the old bazar with its maze of alleyways and squares, wiling away the hours in the cheapest coffee house, where the coffee and tea cost only half a marka.

The gypsy in the coffee house gave him an enquiring look, 'What's wrong with you? You're completely yellow, you should get a doctor to look at you.'

Kamal had seen the dim yellow tint in the mirror but did not know what was wrong. The man insisted he should go to a hospital. Kamal told him he had no papers and that he was not insured. The gypsy treated him to tea and cigarettes and took him to a medical post. In an emergency, they would refer patients to a hospital. Kamal needed a referral, but because he would not be able to produce a certificate of insurance, his chances of getting one were slim. The gypsy told him, 'Just tell them you need the referral, that it's an emergency and that someone else, a brother or something, will come by later to show your passport.'

Kamal asked the staff at the medical post to refer him to the military hospital. They gave him the referral form and told him that he would need to be admitted because of his condition. Kamal returned to the bazar and postponed his hospital visit until that evening. He thought his chances of being admitted would be better if he came in at ten o'clock in the evening. He checked in at the reception and mentioned that somebody would come by with his papers. The doctor on duty quickly realised it would be necessary to take some X-rays. These made it clear Kamal was suffering from jaundice caused by gallstones and an infected gall bladder. He would have to be admitted. First Kamal was treated with medication and given time to recuperate, after which he would be able to have surgery.

He knew the request for his insurance certificate would come. And sure enough, two days later he was asked to present proof of insurance. He bought himself some time by lying again, but he could sense the suspicions of the hospital staff.

The doctors made their rounds every day. Among them was a Syrian who was surprised Kamal could speak Arabic and who enjoyed having a conversation in his own language again. The language created a safe atmosphere in which Kamal was able to tell him he was in trouble, that he had no money or documents and that he did not know what to do. He asked the doctor for help.

The Syrian took action and soon afterwards the medical director showed up at his bedside and asked Kamal about his situation. He told him he would send someone to see if anything could be done. An employee of the national health service visited him and Kamal told her the truth. She tried to get the money from social services, but to no avail. She was unable to help him out. It had become clear to her that Kamal's situation was a blind alley and she told him about a human rights organization in Sarajevo that might be able to help him. She promised to put him in touch with them as soon as he was discharged from hospital.

After six weeks of recuperation, Kamal had the operation. Afterwards, the doctor told him he had removed a spoonful of gallstones. Kamal was allowed to stay at the hospital in order to recover. Inevitably, however, a few weeks later he was back on the streets. It was November 2008, the weather was cold and grey, and winter was on its way.

Vasa Prava was the name of the organization the woman from the national health service had mentioned. It campaigned for civil rights in Bosnia-Herzegovina and offered legal aid. Kamal reported to them and told them his story. He placed his laissez-passer on the table. The temporary travel document from Lebanon was the only thing he had with his name on it. It had not been valid since the late seventies. Nevertheless, Kamal treasured the worthless piece of paper. He had nothing else.

'Come back in a month, we'll see what we can do,' a friendly employee said. Kamal knew how these organizations worked by now and he gave them a little more time. After six weeks he went back to be told they were not ready, that his case was still pending.

'Your file is not complete yet.'

Kamal had started begging again. He had gone back to the coffee house to thank the gypsy for helping him. The man had introduced him to someone who had a place where he could sleep, and maybe even some work. Kamal agreed, but the work turned out to be begging. The man lived off the money the beggars paid him for a place to sleep. So this is what it is like, Kamal thought, you can make a profit even from the poorest of the poor.

When it comes to begging, the trick is to do it without attracting too much attention in a place where there is still a good chance of getting money. The man knew all the best spots and he took Kamal to the Tomb of the Seven Brothers. There was a small mosque there at the edge of the city centre, a famous place of pilgrimage for Muslims who visit Sarajevo. Seven brothers who had risen against their tyrannical father lay in tombs behind the windows. As punishment, their father had sentenced the conspirators to death and, behind each window, a severed head was placed on a tomb. The pilgrims walked around the mosque and tossed a coin through each window. They drank the clear water from the fountain and said a prayer by the graves of regular Muslims outside the building. That was Kamal's spot. He sat on an old chair, a weathered wall behind him, a worn-out man with an impossible dream of an impossible life. He said nothing, apart from the odd 'merci' when someone gave him something. He was not trying to look pathetic, the way he had done by the ATM, he felt too proud for that. But he had succumbed to lethargy, staring blankly for hours as he sat on his rickety chair. He assumed that his mere presence at that place would be understood by the passing pilgrims. Usually he merely nodded his head in thanks for the coins they tossed in the cap by his feet. In this way, he tried to collect enough to pay for his bed and to buy some food. He always hoped for at least ten markas a day. He needed five for the shelter and with another five he would be able to buy some bread, cheese and cigarettes. This was his life, cadging ten markas every day. For people who have never known such a life, it was easy to look down upon those who were living this way.

Many of the faithful who visited Sarajevo had a wish they hoped would be fulfilled if they made a small pilgrimage to three places of worship. First they would visit the Mosque of the Seven Brothers, then the Church of Saint Anthony and finally the Old Orthodox Church. At the mosque they had to say a prayer and at the churches they had to light a candle. A short trip through the city, visiting three holy sites to have their wishes granted. Kamal too decided to try his luck with a few religions and made the trip around the city, against his better judgement, expecting it might help him. That is what they call hope, he would later say, expecting something against your better judgement.

He sometimes thought about his mother and father, as he sat on his chair by the mosque, but he would always hastily suppress the thoughts. He no longer dreamed of a different life, there was no possible escape. He looked for another place to sleep. The owner of his lodgings regarded him as a pariah, tried to profit from his situation and kept asking for more and more money. Kamal had already learned never to tell him how much he had collected each day because the landlord would immediately demand more for the overnight stay. If he made more than ten markas in one day, he kept the extra aside. Some days he would tell him he only had seven markas and that he would not have enough to buy food if he had to pay five for a place to sleep. The landlord never listened. Kamal knew another beggar who slept somewhere else and he told him his landlord was exploiting him. He asked the Roma, called Saban, if he knew of another place or if he could go with him. Saban agreed and Kamal went with him to see where he lived. He arrived at a ruined building that had been abandoned since the war and now housed several Roma. Saban lived in the basement. Kamal was given a room not much bigger than a large cupboard and said, 'How about I pay you fifty markas a month? And please don't ask for more next month, be a friend.'

Saban agreed and Kamal paid him the fifty markas he had saved up by lying to his previous landlord.

∾

Several Roma families lived on the floors above his new abode. He talked to an older woman called Verica who told him that she had been without papers for a long time, but that she would be leaving for Croatia soon. A German woman who was living in Sarajevo had helped her and managed to get her an identity card and a travel permit. She started to tell Kamal her life story, but he was only half listening; he was not interested. All that mattered to him was getting in touch with this German woman. Suddenly he was hopeful that there was somebody who knew of a way out.

'Could you introduce me to her?' Kamal could sense her suspicion. 'And if you don't want to, would you ask her to get in touch with me when you are done with her? Maybe she could do something for me, too.'

Kamal reluctantly explained to her that he did not have any documents either, not even a birth certificate. His income was falling too. Begging was officially prohibited and the authorities had employed a private security company to drive off beggars. He did not like talking about his problems to strangers, but now he had to. He hoped that she would convey the gravity of his situation to the German woman. A few weeks later Verica told him she was going to Croatia soon. Kamal asked her if she had mentioned him.

'Yes, I have told Ingrid about you and she told me she would pay you a visit.'

Kamal did not believe her.

~

So much despair in one single man and nobody cared. Kamal's housemate had left and he was convinced she had lied to him. The German woman never showed up. Week after week he kept on begging and praying to God for salvation. He could not go on, he did not want to go on and he longed for the gun he had carried with him when he was a shepherd.

It was nine o'clock in the morning. Kamal was late and had not yet left to go to his usual begging spot. A girl from one of the Roma families came into the basement and called Kamal.

'Hey grandpa, my mother wants you.'

He went upstairs, annoyed because the little one had called him grandpa.

'Ingrid is here,' the mother said. 'She's the one who helped Verica with the papers to go to Croatia. She wants to see you.'

Kamal was surprised. The German woman had showed up after all. Ingrid explained that she had been told an old man without any papers lived in the house. She claimed she had seen him on a previous visit. Kamal did not recognise her. He did not want his neighbour listening in and asked Ingrid if she spoke English or French. Both languages were fine and Kamal told her his story. Ingrid made notes and asked him for his documents.

'Give me anything you have, it doesn't matter what, so I can make copies.'

Kamal did not have much. He gave her his Lebanese laissez-passer and a few documents he had received at the hospital. The next day she came back, handed back his papers and asked him more about his father and mother, dates of birth, places of birth, dates of death.

He tried to answer her questions as accurately as possible. He had so often been plagued by sudden events that had turned his life upside down and he realised that the good things also seemed to appear when he least expected them. Without realising the full impact of her actions, Ingrid entered his life to turn it all around. It was the summer of 2009 and Kamal felt a new glimmer of hope.

He was pleased to be getting some attention. Finally, he had met someone who cared about his plight. Ingrid worked for a small humanitarian organization from Germany called Pharos. She mostly worked on other projects, but the desperate situation of those who were stateless had deeply moved her, and she made every effort to help them in her free time.

The first thing Ingrid did was to get in touch with Vasa Prava, the human rights organization Kamal had turned to after his stay at the hospital. The organization offered help and legal advice to refugees, asylum seekers and 'internally displaced persons', people in the Balkans who, after the war, had found themselves in a country they did not consider their homeland. Ingrid made a phone call to the woman who had looked at Kamal's case. Her reply was sobering. The file was on her desk, she had not had time to look into it and, quite frankly, they did not really know what they could do for him.

Shortly afterwards Ingrid visited Kamal again. She showed him some printouts with information about his father she had found on the internet. Kamal glanced over the text. He read that Zvonimir Kojadin had been the head of department II of a branch of the Croatian intelligence service and that he had been responsible for all intelligence activity directed against foreign intelligence services, international freemasonry, political activists and Croatian emigrants in general. For the first time, he read about the things his father had never been willing to discuss with him, about his role in intelligence and counterintelligence. It was confirmation of his father's role in Pavelic's regime during the war, and it was clear why the Egyptians had wanted his father so badly for their intelligence service. Not long after, she came by with his father's birth certificate. She had requested a copy in Travnik and received one without any difficulty.

'You can look for your mother's birth certificate yourself here in Sarajevo,' she had said.

Kamal told her he had tried before. He did have another idea, though. He had not yet searched for his parents' marriage certificate, though he knew they had got married in Sarajevo.

He proudly presented Ingrid with the copy. It had been a long time since he had felt so full of energy. He had managed to find his parents' marriage certificate. Sadeta Adinovic and Zvonimir Kojadin married in Sarajevo on 31 August 1941. He had the proof. At the archives of the registry of births, marriages and deaths he had again been told that his mother's birth certificate was missing.

'It's no use, Ingrid,' Kamal said. 'You won't find anything in Zagreb.'

Ingrid wanted to inquire after his birth certificate in Croatia. She thought it was important, even if there was no certificate.

'We have to build a case file. Let them officially say they don't have anything, that they didn't register your birth.'

Kamal relented and with her help he wrote and signed the request. Finding out where to send the letter was quite a puzzle in itself. Weeks later the formal reply arrived. It came as no surprise: he was not registered.

'That means we will have to go further back,' Ingrid said. 'We'll find out which hospital you were born in and if you were registered there.'

She got the relevant phone numbers from a friend in Zagreb, but this line of inquiry also proved fruitless. Nothing could be found in any of the archives about a child with the name Kojadin being born on 22 October 1944.

The UN refugee agency has an office in Sarajevo, and Kamal went there with Ingrid. She did not know what their next step should be and was hoping for some tips from UNHCR. They had trouble finding out who they should talk to. Kamal could not remember how many times he had told his story by now. The UNHCR employee had a new idea. He assumed Kamal must have been baptised because his father was a Catholic. He promised to have someone check the records of the churches in Zagreb for his baptism certificate. Kamal thought they would get an answer soon, within ten days, he hoped. But weeks passed and in the end it turned out that UNHCR had not done anything yet.

'Then we will just keep on trying ourselves,' Ingrid said.

Twice they had relied on an organization and both times they had ended up on a waiting list. Ingrid had had enough of waiting in vain. Kamal knew how this would end. He knew that these organizations that opened their door to people would eventually close it again. He knew that even sympathetic people soon realised they did not know what to do, and often drowned in the workload. The same was true of the International Organization for Migration. They also employed lawyers, experts in the field of legal and illegal migrants, but even they could not say what Kamal and Ingrid should do in the case of an unregistered adult.

Ingrid went back to the registry in Sarajevo with his father's birth certificate and his parents' marriage certificate in an attempt to get

Kamal's birth registered retrospectively. Again they told her nothing could be done without a birth certificate.

'But he doesn't have one,' Ingrid told them.

'Then I don't know what to do, either', the civil servant replied. 'We need it as proof.'

Kamal had known it for a long time and Ingrid was now finding out, to her own frustration, that a birth certificate is the key to every door. Ingrid checked it at every possible level of administration in Bosnia-Herzegovina: the government of the canton, the federation and the state. Nobody was authorised or responsible, and all doors remained firmly closed to them.

'It's not just their doors they have closed, Kamal, they have closed their hearts as well.'

~

'This might be our only chance', Ingrid said to Kamal.

She simply could not let go of the idea the employee at UNHCR had mentioned about the baptism certificate. She asked around and got the name of a priest of a Catholic congregation in the Marjin Dvor district of Sarajevo. Kamal and Ingrid visited him and asked them what they would have to do to get their hands on the certificate. It would be impossible to search all the churches in Zagreb themselves. The priest was immediately willing to help them and he knew the solution. He submitted an episcopal request and managed to get people to search the records of all the churches in Zagreb. The result came back some weeks later. Negative, nobody had found anything. Apparently, Kamal had not been baptised at that time. It had been his last hope. He knew who his father and mother had been, but it remained uncertain who he was himself.

How important it is to know somebody who knows somebody. Kamal smiled. Ingrid was persistent and he admired her for it. She had got in touch with an acquaintance who knew an employee at a UN organization in Zagreb. There was nothing the employee could do for Kamal but he did put him in touch with the human rights ombudsman of the Republic of Croatia. There, they requested documents from his former place of residence, Opatija. Kamal was known to the authorities there and they had a file on him. Months later, the file arrived at the ombudsman's office.

Ingrid called him. 'I think you might have a chance, Kamal.' She had driven to Zagreb to meet with the ombudsman. 'I think you might be able to get Croatian nationality.'

Kamal's file contained a document with his personal information from the time when he had had residency in Croatia, in 1993 and 1994. Ingrid had discussed it with the ombudsman and had got the impression it might be possible for Kamal to obtain Croatian citizenship, because it was likely he had been born in Zagreb, even though the document stated 'no nationality'.

It took a while before their hope proved false once more. The ombudsman had taken a closer look at the file and had decided that there were no grounds on which Kamal could acquire Croatian nationality because there was no evidence that he had been born on Croatian territory.

It was yet another way of saying it was impossible to obtain citizenship without a birth certificate. Refugees and asylum seekers were often marked 'nationality unknown'. This meant they had a nationality, but that the nature of it was unknown. This seemed an easy situation to Kamal, as in such cases the unknown simply had to become known. His papers, however, clearly stated 'no nationality'. For Kamal, it was just further confirmation that, officially, he did not exist.

He was back at square one. But the ombudsman had given him an important tip. He advised Kamal to submit a written request for registration as a citizen with the relevant authorities. Only then would a procedure be set in motion, because the government is obliged to respond such a request. Ingrid also discovered that in most countries a person can acquire the nationality of a state if one of the parents has the nationality of that country. International law dictates that everyone is entitled to a nationality and Ingrid had read that in Yugoslavia and the states of former Yugoslavia the jus sanguini system applies, a legal principle based on the right of blood. This means a child will get the nationality of its parents. But which organization was responsible in Kamal's case? Ingrid promised Kamal she would get to the bottom of it.

'It's complicated, Kamal,' she told him.

Since the Dayton Agreement had been signed in 1995 the Republic of Bosnia-Herzegovina had consisted of two federal states: the Federation of Bosnia and Herzegovina, and the Serbian Republic. Kamal's father's birthplace, Travnik, was in the former.

'That's where you should submit your request, Kamal, with the Federation, I think they are authorised.'

Ingrid sent the request in Kamal's name and after a few more weeks of waiting, the answer arrived. The Ministry of Interior of the Federation believed it did not have authority in the matter and its officials were of the opinion that he could not be awarded citizenship because he did not have a birth certificate to prove who he was. They had come full circle again.

It seemed like a good idea to Ingrid if Kamal signed a proxy statement so she could act freely in his name. Arranging this proved difficult. They needed a notary who was willing to accept witnesses who would confirm his identity. Not every notary was satisfied with the witnesses Kamal came up with, two gypsies from his shelter. In the end it was Ingrid who found someone willing to do it. Kamal signed the document so Ingrid could continue the search without him. He was exhausted and had trouble walking. The endless rounds of offices and reception desks were taking their toll.

~

'He is living on the streets, he is ill and he is begging for a living, he cannot go on like this much longer!'

Ingrid told Kamal she had lost her temper. It was early 2010 and, because of her positive experiences with the ombudsman in Croatia, she had contacted the Bosnian ombudsman, who defended the rights of citizens in the face of bureaucracy there. He had said he would note the details of Kamal's case, and let her know when his case came up for consideration. Ingrid had a feeling this would take a very long time and she had had words with the man. She had pleaded with him until he agreed to get onto the case directly. With his help, she found out that Kamal had to submit his request to another organization, the Ministry of Internal Affairs of the sub-district where Travnik was situated. Ingrid had already submitted a request to the Federation. However, the ombudsman surmised that authority lay not with the Federation, but with the canton. Kamal sighed, as did Ingrid, and then they sent their umpteenth signed request.

~

The official documents were written in a largely unfathomable language. Nevertheless, Ingrid had found out there was such a thing as a right of residence on humanitarian grounds in Bosnia-Herzegovina.

'I am now talking about the Republic of Bosnia-Herzegovina, of which the Federation is only a part,' she explained to Kamal. 'It might be possible to get you a residence permit here in Bosnia.'

There are several grounds on which a person can obtain a residence permit. A permit can be granted because of work or marriage, but in Kamal's case Ingrid submitted the request on humanitarian grounds. Her supporting argument was that Kamal needed health insurance. As a foreigner in Bosnia, he could only obtain insurance if he had a residence permit. It took months, and still Kamal did not get any reply.

'How hard can it be? I am going to take it to the ombudsman,' Ingrid cried angrily.

The ombudsman lodged an objection in Kamal's name, on the grounds that he had not received an answer in the specified time. It worked. Suddenly, they received word within five days; the permit had been granted. For Kamal, it took a while for the idea to sink in. It was the first official recognition of his existence. He took a deep breath. The moment he had been waiting for was finally here. From now on he would be able to prove who he was.

The serial number on the ID card that Kamal proudly held in his hand was 000001. It was July 2010 and Kamal Kojadin was the first person in Bosnia-Herzegovina without a nationality to receive a temporary residence permit and an accompanying ID card on humanitarian grounds. The ID was the size of a credit card with a biometric passport photo.

The permit, which would be valid until March 2011, allowed Kamal to apply for health insurance for the first time in his life. Pharos, the humanitarian organization Ingrid worked for, was willing to pay the sixty markas in insurance premium each month. It was a big step forward. In the eyes of the authorities, Kamal was still a man with no nationality, a foreigner, but he did have an identity.

~

'Are you saying there might be a file on you in Bihac?' Ingrid exclaimed in surprise.

Kamal nodded his head. He rarely thought about it. He sometimes had coffee with Ingrid and she would often ask him about his life. Bit by bit he told her, including about the time he lived in Bihac, where the local police, through the Centre for Aliens, had contacted the Ministry of Foreign Affairs in Lebanon to validate Kamal's story. A document from Interpol in his file in Bihac might prove crucial. It was a letter from his parents in which they confirmed they had a son called Kamal. His fingerprint was attached to this letter.

Ingrid did not consider her work done. Kamal did not have citizenship of any country and was still unable to claim entitlements to any services. She contacted the Centre for Aliens and soon found out how important her discovery was. The rejection letter they had received from the Ministry of Internal Affairs stated there was no confirmation of Kamal's identity. Ingrid now knew this confirmation did exist, in Bihac. There was just one more problem: the Centre for Aliens did not want to give it to her formally, in writing, because the organization Ingrid worked for was not registered. These kinds of document could only be obtained through official channels. Again, it took weeks before the proof was sent from Bihac to the authorities in Sarajevo. Ingrid did not get to see this important letter, but the relevant authorities did. On the grounds of this document, Kamal's identity was officially established.

Ingrid had submitted the request concerning Kamal's citizenship to the canton where Travnik was situated in early 2010, on the advice of the ombudsman. It had been received and processed and more than six months later, in August 2010, it was rejected. The canton had also found no grounds on which to grant citizenship to Kamal. He did, however, have the option of appealing against this decision, within fourteen days.

'I am not a lawyer,' Ingrid said, 'and I can't find one who is specialised in such cases and who would be able to appeal.'

'Never mind,' Kamal answered. 'It's useless, I am a son of the Ustaše, that's why they are against us.'

Ingrid was angry and desperate. She had tried without success to find support at UNHCR in Belgrade. But she refused to give up, and had another look at Kamal's letter of rejection. One of the arguments put forth was the fact that Kamal's father did not have Bosnian-Herzegovinian nationality. He was not in the population register, but he was in the register of births in Travnik. These were two separate registers, and according to the officials, that meant Kamal's father did not have Bosnian citizenship. Ingrid studied all the literature about statelessness and the international conventions related to the subject. There was an abundance of information. She discovered that Kamal's father was not stateless according to the law – 'de jure' – but only in practice – 'de facto' – and that is a major difference. Kamal's father was born in Travnik, in 1910, in a state that was the predecessor of what is present-day Bosnia-Herzegovina. In international law, certain rules apply when it comes to state succession. People affected by state succession may not be rendered stateless. Therefore, countries must ensure that policies concerning nationality are adapted in such a way that no one ends up stateless. In Yugoslavia, this proved difficult, because the country had fallen apart into several states. This did not change the fact that residents of former Yugoslavia had the right to obtain citizenship of one of the successor states, however.

'Kamal, your father never renounced his citizenship, did he? And it was never officially taken away from him, even though he was never on Bosnian territory after the war?'

It was a statement rather than a question. In her eyes, Ingrid had found the crucial argument. Legally, Kamal's father had Bosnian nationality, because he had been born in an area that was now part of Bosnia, she thought, which would mean the canton's decision was incorrect. Kamal agreed with her.

～

The appeal against the canton's decision had to be submitted within fourteen days. Ingrid was in a hurry and she channelled all her anger and frustration at the indifference of the organizations into setting up the appeal. She immersed herself in the information she had collected after they had received the rejection, ploughed through international conventions and often worked late into night. She thought she had found the grounds on which Kamal would have to be granted citizenship.

It came as a surprise when, at that very moment, a UNHCR official in Sarajevo contacted her concerning the request for legal assistance that she had submitted earlier to a department of the refugee organization in Belgrade. That very same day she met with UNHCR staff. She had completed the appeal. The lawyers looked at the letter and had nothing to add. Ingrid was proud of her legal work, conducted without any legal training. The appeal was sent to the canton.

It was late 2010 when a motorcycle drew up in front of Kamal's home. He saw Ingrid and her husband Ilja dismount and remove their helmets. Ingrid took a blue envelope from the pocket of her leather jacket and brought it inside.

'We have come to have a drink with you, Kamal, because we have cause for celebration.' She quoted from the letter she had received from the ministry in Travnik: '...we hereby respond to your appeal and inform you that your entry in the register of births has been approved retrospectively. This decision is final.' For a moment, her words did not quite register with Kamal. Then it dawned on him that, even though he was 66 at this point, he had officially been born on 14 December 2010.

Kamal and Ingrid looked at each other as they raised their glasses.

'Cheers, Kamal, here's to your second birth!'

Kamal travelled to Travnik to express his gratitude. The letter in the blue envelope had stated that the Ministry's earlier decision had been declared null and void and that the proposed arguments were valid. On those grounds, Kamal's name had been entered in the register of births. Kamal wanted to meet the officials who had confirmed this.

'It was complicated for us as well,' one of them said.

It turned out they were not up to scratch when it came to international conventions and had had to go to a law library to study the matter. Luckily, Bosnia-Herzegovina was one of the countries where international conventions took precedence over national law, under the terms of the Dayton Agreement, the peace treaty that had brought the civil war in Bosnia to an end.

'You have created a precedent,' the official said. Kamal raised his eyebrows. All that mattered to him was his own brand new birth certificate.

The bureaucracy was no longer any impediment. With his birth certificate, ID card, two passport photographs and a hundred markas, he visited the Aliens Police. Fourteen days later, he received the first identification card in Bosnia-Herzegovina issued under the terms of international law. A little later, he applied for a passport, and this request was granted too. He walked into a bank and asked at the desk if he could open an account. It was a strange experience. Something that had been impossible his entire life could now be arranged in a few minutes.

Ingrid drew up a contract confirming that Kamal would be employed by her organization. He was assigned to represent Pharos in its dealings with the authorities and to do what Ingrid had done for him. He was to mediate for the many people in Sarajevo who were stateless. His salary amounted to two hundred euros, the equivalent of four hundred Bosnian markas, which was enough to live off. A black briefcase and a stack of business cards, and Kamal was back on his feet.

~

Ingrid had a contact who helped her with her work in Foca, a small village a few miles away in Bosnia. He was looking for a place to live and Ingrid found a small house that suited him. The man turned it down. Kamal was still sleeping in the cupboard-like room in Saban's basement. Ingrid knew about his situation and she contacted him.

'I might have found a place for you to live, Kamal. Go to the TV tower and call this number when you get there. Somebody who can show you the place will come and pick you up.'

Kamal had a look at the place. It consisted of two small rooms, both in bad repair. It lacked proper sanitary facilities and storage space. It was not great, but it was affordable, a hundred and twenty markas rent and another thirty for electricity. He took it willingly. Anything would be better than what he had and besides, he did not want to offend Ingrid. The biggest drawback was having to commute. From the centre of Sarajevo he could take a bus to the foot of the hill and, from there, make the climb uphill on foot for about half an hour. This was very difficult for him, since he had trouble walking due to arteriosclerosis.

~

Kamal started working for Pharos in the spring of 2011. It soon proved difficult. His conversations with the Roma were laborious. Kamal had friends who were Roma, had had many dealings with them and had even lived amongst them. Still, his experiences with these nomadic people had been predominantly bad. The work was hard. Promises were broken, he was lied to and children were scared of him. He did not dare tell Ingrid, whom he revered and who had done so much for him.

Ingrid asked him to start looking for a certain Kemo, a Roma she had been in touch with for a little while, but who had vanished from sight. Based on her information, Kamal distributed adverts throughout the city. A few weeks later, Ingrid told him they had been successful and together they visited Kemo. Gradually, their communication improved and Kamal finally saw his chance to have a word with Ingrid, which he had been putting off for a while. He thought Kemo could take over from him.

'Listen, Ingrid, the work doesn't really suit me. I can't deal with them and they don't trust me. I think Kemo would do a better job.'

'I know, Kamal, but I was waiting for you to come to me about it.'

'It just isn't working with these people, Ingrid. I know there are exceptions to the rule, but I have got to know them. They have no regard for the law or for common decency. They lie and they cheat. Every generation says they don't want their children to live the same life, yet they never change.'

Kamal resigned and Kemo took over. With that, Kamal's contract with Pharos expired and he no longer received the two hundred euros every month. As soon as Kamal had been awarded his citizenship, a year of waiting had commenced before he could claim any rights as regards housing and social services in the canton of Sarajevo. By now, the year had passed and Kamal submitted a welfare application. He soon received monthly benefits of two hundred markas, which paid his rent. With a small financial contribution from the German aid organization, he was just about able to support himself.

~

He was shy, and so was his son. And so, after all these years, they simply sat across from one another. Ingrid had got in touch with his sons and given them his phone number. Leo, the middle one, called and said he wanted to meet him. He came from Belgrade, half a day's journey from Sarajevo. Kamal felt uncomfortable. How would his son feel about him? He had not been in touch with him for so long. What kind of ideas and beliefs would he have? After all, he had been raised an Orthodox Catholic in Serbia. What kind of values had been imprinted on him since his childhood? Prejudices from both sides made for a laborious start to the conversation. Leo was reserved because the stories he had heard from other people had given him a negative image of his father. Kamal was supposedly a warmongering smuggler, a man involved in all kinds of illegal business. Leo mostly had a lot of questions and Kamal answered them circumspectly but truthfully, hoping his son would see he was an honest man. Leo asked about his mother. He wanted to know what she had been like and how she had died. Kamal realised his son barely knew anything about his mother and he talked at length about her, omitting only the time of her alcohol addiction. He asked his son if he knew where Majda's grave was located. Leo told him he still visited the place now and then, which is how Kamal knew his wife's grave in Grocka was still there. He did not have a photograph of her and he promised his son that, if he got a chance, he would go to Croatia, visit Majda's brother and ask him for a picture.

Leo left for Belgrade again. He had asked Kamal what would be a good souvenir to take with him from Sarajevo. Kamal had answered that about ninety percent of all souvenirs would be Islamic and might not go down well with his adoptive parents. Together they had laughed about this precarious issue of faith and Kamal felt it no longer stood between them after this meeting. Leo decided it would be best to take a bottle of rakia.

~

They did not see each other again after this meeting. Leo had to prepare for exams. He called again after the summer to say he had graduated. Adam, too, the eldest of his three sons, called him in the spring of 2012. It was a short conversation. 'There was too much distance between us,' Kamal said later, and it made him sad. He noticed that his sons were ambitious and wanted to get on in life, but that they were poor. They wanted a better life and Kamal could not offer them anything as their father. He had explained this to Leo, that he was unable to do anything for them, that he had only just received papers, was only just able to identify himself for the first time, and maybe start a small business. He would have liked to promise them something, to offer them some prospects, but deep inside, he felt it was too late for him to have any kind of future. Alan, the youngest, was the last to call him. He said he had to finish his studies before meeting him.

'I will be finished next year, then I want to see you, all three of us will come visit you together.'

'That's great, call me when you're coming,' Kamal said. 'I'll wait for you at the station.'

2012 - 2014, SARAJEVO, BRUSSELS, ANTWERP, EPILOGUE

What Kamal had told me on the plaza stayed in my mind and a year after our first meeting, I decided to write his story. I called him, he agreed and we arranged to meet for a long interview. In November 2012 I spent ten days with him in Sarajevo. We would sit at the table together every day and, bit by bit, we pieced the story of his life together. Usually, the conversation started off in English. When emotions came into it, Kamal would switch to French, a language he felt more at ease with. Sometimes, we would puzzle over a word and I would ask Kamal if he knew the German for it. Sometimes we had to look up an actual translation.

There were times when I found it hard to believe Kamal as he told me about the extraordinary turns his life had taken. There were times when we argued, like when Kamal bluntly spoke his mind about the Roma, or when he downplayed the horrors at the Jasenovac concentration camp, which his father must have been aware of. He claimed it had not been as bad as Auschwitz, because no one had been killed in gas chambers. There were moments, too, when Kamal would sit, staring at the wall, warily searching for words to paint a picture of his imprisonment, his destiny and his unfulfilled desires.

'The eye sees more than the hand can grasp. That is how it has always been for me. I saw it, I wanted it, but I could not reach it.'

Having insisted several times, I finally visited Kamal's little house on the hill. I wanted to see how he lived, to see him in his little home up the hill.

'It's out of my hands,' Kamal said. 'I have nowhere to put my clothes.' He was embarrassed about the chaotic, unhygienic, drab little space he lived in. He admitted he made a mess and that he actually needed a woman to keep the place clean and tidy for him.

After more than a week of interviews, we said our goodbyes.

'What was it like for you, Kamal?'

'It was like therapy,' Kamal confided to me. He felt liberated by exploring his life the way we had. I distinctly remember his answer when I told him that I considered the time he had talked to me as work on his part, and that I wanted to pay him for it. He accepted my money with the well-chosen words, 'If it feels good for you, it feels good for me.'

Kamal made his first journey with a valid passport in June 2013. He took the bus from Sarajevo to Opatija. In the past he had crossed Yugoslavia from Belgrade to Opatija without any hindrance. After the war, there was a border between Bosnia and Croatia that he could not pass without papers. It felt strange to him. He finally had his coveted passport and now he had to use it go to a place he had visited many times without any problem when he had been stateless.

I had rented a holiday home in Pobri, the part of Opatija where

Kamal had lived himself. We had arranged to visit several places together. He was hoping to retrieve some of his lost memories and to visit old friends, and I wanted to get a better picture of what his life had been like and of the place that had played such a significant role in his story. The first day after his arrival in Opatija, he went in search of his old friends. He let me drive him up the mountain close to Ika, a little south of Opatija. That had been the location of the restaurant owned by the Dervisevic family, where he had lived and worked when he arrived in Yugoslavia from Switzerland. He unerringly guided me up a series of meandering roads. It turned out the restaurant had been shut down. Ali Dervisevic's second wife still lived there and rented out rooms to students at the Faculty of Tourism and Hospitality Management in Opatija. Ali was the one who had fled Rome and ended up in Beirut. Kamal had often been in touch with him and they had worked together for a while. Ali had left a restless Beirut a little while after Kamal and, after a period in Turkey, had ended up back with his family in Yugoslavia. His wife said her husband had died of lung cancer in 2003. Ali had been operated on in Turkey, but had stopped breathing after five days in a coma. Kamal did not know about this. Ahmed, who had received him so hospitably and who had taken him in and employed him as a cook, was also dead. He had suffered a fatal stroke in 2009. None of this news had reached Kamal at the time, when he had been roaming the hills around Bihac as a shepherd and begging in Sarajevo. But there was more bad news. The Dervisevic brothers had had two cousins. At the time, both had been part of Kamal's circle of friends and now they were dead too. Pensively nodding and with a face void of expression, Kamal sat on the terrace of the former restaurant under the cherry trees he had planted himself. Everyone was dead and nothing was as it had been.

'I need help, I'm tired.' Kamal caught my arm and linked it with his own for support. The arteries in his legs did not allow him to walk more than a hundred metres before he needed to rest again. So I walked with him, stopping frequently along the boulevard in Opatija. Kamal used the breaks to point out the places he had told me about. The low wall where he had displayed his wares, the narrow window ledge of the kiosk across the road where he sat waiting for customers. The Admiral Hotel, the construction of which had driven him and Smelia away from their good spot. The place where he had first spotted Doris Day. Those were the places he recognised. Other than that, hardly anything was the same. Terraces had disappeared, new buildings had sprung up, natural stone had made way for tarmac and concrete. Weary and short of breath, the prematurely aged Kamal walked beside me through the streets of Opatija, shaking his head, mumbling how everything had changed. He had been looking forward to revisiting the past, but was now completely disillusioned.

In the evenings we sat on the terrace of our rented house. Kamal stared at the hills and the sea, which was just visible in the distance. I did not know what was going on inside his head, but I thought I saw regret and melancholy.

Kamal used his tatty mobile to call several old acquaintances, all to no avail. 'The number you have called is not in service', 'Leave a message after the beep and I'll call you back', 'This number cannot be reached'. He was not making any progress. At last, I heard him speaking to someone. It turned out to be an acquaintance of Slavitza, the woman he had lived with during the war in Croatia. Slavitza was on holiday, however, so this proved to be another dead end.

When we said goodbye to each other in November 2012, I made a promise to Kamal. He had set his hopes on having his arteriosclerosis treated by Arab doctors in Belgium. His friend

Hassan who had left Bihac and now lived in Brussels had assured him that the doctors there would undoubtedly be willing to operate on him. Kamal did not have much faith in the Bosnian healthcare system and had mentioned several times that he wanted to go to Belgium for treatment. Ingrid had always replied that he should really quit smoking and live a healthier life. I got the feeling he did not think this would solve his problems. I promised him I would pay for a plane ticket to Belgium on condition that he got in touch with Hassan, whom he had not spoken to for a long time, to find out if he was willing to take him in. In the months that followed Kamal did not manage to contact Hassan.

The first sign of hope was a meeting we had with Hassan's son. He was living with his mother, Hassan's ex-wife, in an apartment in Opatija. I took Kamal to the address and got to know the son. He gave us Hassan's Skype address. The second spark of hope came when an old friend of Kamal's returned his phone call at the last minute. They would meet at the bus station in Rijeka, a few hours before Kamal was to take the bus back to Sarajevo. I drove him there and witnessed two old friends greeting each other. I also saw something I had not seen before: Kamal as he must have been a long time ago.

It was Kamal's youngest son Alan who had promised to contact him and had told him that the three brothers would come to Sarajevo together. So Kamal waited. Ingrid called him passive and had become quite annoyed at what she considered his lazy way of attributing everything that happened to the will of God.

'If you can roll a cigarette, you can put a stamp on an envelope!' she exclaimed and then went on to say that she would take the initiative. That summer I learned of her resolve to arrange a meeting between Kamal and his sons in September. I was keen to know the outcome and by the end of September 2013, I sent her a message saying I hoped she had succeeded. Not much later, I received her reply; the meeting had not taken place. She had not managed to get in touch with Alan. His phone had been constantly out of service and he did not reply to her emails. Kamal thanked her for the efforts she had made for him.

'Maybe it's all too late, Ingrid.'

~

'Kamal landed at Zaventem airport around eight o'clock on Wednesday evening. Yesterday we spoke on Skype and I saw him sitting on the sofa next to Hassan with that charming smile we all know so well. I am hoping to visit him sometime next week,' I wrote in an email to Ingrid on 8 November 2013.

When I got in touch with him, using the contact details his son had given me, it turned out Hassan was willing to receive Kamal with open arms and to arrange for the coveted doctor's appointment.

On 6 November 2013 an Adria Airways plane with Kamal Kojadin on board landed at Zaventem airport. He had flown from Sarajevo via Ljubljana to Brussels. Later he told me that, on the way to arrivals, he had taken some deep breaths. He added with a wink that they contained more oxygen. For the first time, he was outside camp Yugoslavia and he felt liberated. He had a Schengen visa that would allow him to stay in Belgium for three months.

Later that month, I parked my car in the Molenbeek neighbourhood, the area where Hassan lived, depicted by the media as a bulwark of Salafists and an international breeding ground for jihadists and foreign fighters in Syria. I was clearly the exception in the streets full of djellabas and burkas. I climbed several flights of stairs and was welcomed with tea, fruit and biscuits. It was a pleasant meeting that left me none the wiser about Kamal's highly recommended Arab doctors who would cure the afflictions brought on by his arteriosclerosis. We agreed to keep in touch by Skype and after several hours I left the small, dingy male household.

Shortly afterwards, I heard Kamal had been examined by a medical specialist who had prescribed medication. Hassan told me the doctor had given Kamal a prescription. The doctor had explained that an operation might be necessary, but that he would not be able to claim the high costs on Hassan's health insurance

'I'm working on something, though. I can't tell you what it is yet. I'll let you know,' Hassan promised me at the end of our conversation.

In the conversations that followed he repeated this message. He maintained his mysterious demeanour even when it became clear to me that Kamal was no longer living at the apartment in Brussels.

'He's in a clinic.'

That was all I got. Hassan did not elaborate, although I pressed for more details and said I thought it unlikely that, in the Belgium healthcare system, someone would be admitted to a clinic for treatment as simple as cholesterol-lowering statins. Kamal had already been there for fourteen days. After repeated questioning, Hassan finally admitted that Kamal was in Antwerp.

'Then give me his mobile number. I would like to talk to him myself.'

'I'll ask Kamal to call you.'

'Fine,' I answered.

It was clear to me that something was going on that Hassan did not want me to know about. Kamal called me and went along with the story. He claimed to be in some kind of hospital for treatment and said he was getting medication every day and needed regular check-ups. The murmur in the background did nothing to convince me that he was actually in a clinic.

'I want to visit Kamal, Hassan. Antwerp is close, give me his address.'

This was my next attempt to find out what was really going on.

'I'll ask Kamal to come to the station, so you can pick him up there.'

Another attempt by Hassan to conceal the truth from me. I suggested a date, and Hassan said he would arrange the get-together. A few days later I got a call from Kamal.

'It's easier if I pick you up at the clinic, Kamal, then we can drive into the city together to catch up.'

Kamal agreed and explicitly said he would wait by the road at the agreed time. He obviously did not want me at the clinic either. Finally, he gave me the address. I did a quick online search and everything soon became clear. Kamal was at the Linkeroever Red Cross refugee centre in Antwerp.

The man who had lived without an identity for so long and now finally owned a passport had left the document in a drawer at Hassan's and reported to the authorities as a refugee without papers. It gave him the right to medical treatment.

> *'Season's greetings from Kamal. I saw him in Antwerp last Saturday. He is staying there now for medical treatment. He says it is working. It seemed to me he is walking better than last summer in Opatija, so perhaps the medication really is working (and he only smokes five cigarettes a day, or so he claims).'*

I chose not to mention any details. Kamal had told me over coffee what had happened. He had used the war in Syria and the fact that he spoke Arabic fluently to his advantage and had registered as a refugee in Brussels. His story was that he had fled from a small village in the Homs area, where a large group of civilians had been caught up in the fighting between the rebels and the Syrian army in the summer of 2013. He told the Belgians he had fled along what would later become known as the 'Balkan route', an escape route he had taken illegally by truck from Turkey, via Bulgaria and straight through Serbia to Western Europe. They deemed it a plausible story and he was referred to the Red Cross refugee centre in Antwerp, which had a place available. Kamal showed me the 'immatriculation certificate' he had received in Antwerp, complete with stamps and his photograph. In Belgium that was the official name for what was in fact nothing more than a registration certificate. It was made out to 'Kamal XXXX, no occupation, born in Tal Kalakh, Syria (Arab Republic)', a small town to the west of Homs and not far from the Lebanese border that is inhabited mainly by Muslims. The document was valid until early March 2014 and it stated clearly that it was in no way an identification document nor a certificate of nationality.

'A refugee centre, Kamal? You don't know anybody there and you only get pills that you could also get anywhere else.'

Kamal disagreed.

'It's better than being alone on a mountain top in Sarajevo,' he replied. 'And if I need an operation, I can get one for free.'

He did not mind the place, he got hot meals, had lots of people to talk to and an important role in the group because of his language skills.

Kamal had adjusted his goals. Those who were given asylum in Belgium subsequently got the right to housing and could apply for benefits. What had been an attempt to obtain free medical care now became a hunt for an asylum permit that would allow him to stay in Belgium permanently; it was preferable to remaining a foreigner in the country of his birth.

Once again, Kamal reverted to his past in Lebanon and the knowledge that it was not who you are, but who you know that can make a difference when you need it. Sitting across from me in the café in Antwerp, he asked me if I knew any freemasons. I did not, but I promised to do some research and on New Year's Day 2014 I sent an email to the local masonic lodge. Two weeks later I received a reply.

> 'I have received your email and have contacted him. He says he is a Syrian who was a member of a lodge there 40 years ago, which was disbanded by the regime. It is difficult for us to check. Apparently he is an old man. We do not want to give him false hope that we are able to help him. I assume there must be organizations there that are in a better position to help, and we are willing to support them within our limited means. If you are part of such an organization, we would be happy to hear from you.'

The brothers and sisters of the network he had pinned his hopes on had let him down.

~

The visa with which Kamal had entered the European Union early in November was valid for three months. He had told me he would like to return to Belgium to continue the asylum procedure he had set in motion. I did not want to stand in the way of that and provided him with a return ticket. On 29 January, he would fly back to Sarajevo via Vienna, and a week later he would return to Brussels.

Ingrid warned me this would not be possible under European law. In hindsight, she turned out to be right. Officially, the visa Kamal had been granted was a permit, issued by a Schengen state, allowing the holder to pass through or remain on the territory of that member state for no more than a total of three months over a six-month period.

However, Hassan had been in touch with a friend in Bosnia who claimed that it would be possible for him to return on the planned date, 5 January. Kamal was willing to risk it, in his desperate attempt to become a recognised asylum seeker.

> *'Kamal will fly this Wednesday. I am sending you a copy of the ticket so you can see when he will arrive. As you are aware, Kamal wants to try to return to Belgium by any means. It is up to him to decide. I am not certain it will work. Perhaps you could talk to him when he is back in Sarajevo about the sense of all this? We shall see, and let's keep in touch.'*

Ingrid had asked an acquaintance of Kamal's to pick him up at the airport. On the day Kamal was to fly from Zaventem to Sarajevo, I received her reply.

> *'Kamal's contact Christof waited for him at the airport at 14.15. Kamal was not on board. Do you have any idea what happened?'*

A day later, I got in touch with Hassan on Skype. Kamal had missed his plane, he claimed. I am still uncertain whether Kamal did this on purpose to eliminate the possibility of flying into camp Yugoslavia and not being allowed to leave again. The fact remained that from that moment on, Kamal was living in Belgium illegally and had degraded himself to a citizen with no rights, after so many years and so much effort to escape that situation.

On 19 April 2014 I sent Ingrid an email.

> *'Kamal departed this morning with a delay of 45 minutes. Hassan has been in touch with his landlord who has agreed to pick him up*

tomorrow when he arrives around 15.30. I hope for him that everything goes well.'

Not long after Kamal had decided to continue the asylum procedure, it became clear during an in-depth interview with the immigration services that he was unable to provide convincing answers to certain crucial questions about Talkalakh, his supposed place of birth in Syria. His asylum request was denied and he had just a few weeks to leave the country. He spent a little more time at Hassan's before he departed from the Brussels-North bus station, heading for Sarajevo. He returned to the city of his mother's birth, to the land of his father that would never be his fatherland. This had been his final attempt to escape the Balkans. Kamal was going home.

ACKNOWLEDGMENTS

Literary non-fiction is a genre that does not give the writer much creative freedom. Although the pen of the author might colour the writing, the reader expects a true account of what actually happened.

When it came to the story of Kamal Kojadin, the material I got from the interviews in Sarajevo was all I had to work with. Of course, I have asked myself whether some – maybe even many – aspects of his life story were fictional. Did Kamal just have a wild imagination?

When I was doing my research in preparation for writing this book, I checked every fact, meeting and name Kamal had told me about to the best of my ability. None turned out to be false. I consider this fact-checking exercise a kind of random sampling, and based on that I have concluded that the events of Kamal's life did indeed happen as he related them to me.

The second confirmation that his story is indeed true relates to the chapters on Bihac and Sarajevo, where I had the opportunity to compare Kamal's story with the interviews I conducted with

Hassan and Ingrid respectively. Naturally, their stories were told from a different perspective, were coloured differently, but the events corresponded.

Ingrid was able to read the Sarajevo chapter because I had it translated into German, as part of my efforts to ensure the greatest possible factual accuracy. All her comments pertained to details which to some extent were simply misinterpretation on my part. Language and translation were also complicating factors. Kamal and I conversed mostly in English and French. Ingrid gave me her account in German.

In short, I believe the extraordinary story of Kamal's life, set against the backdrop of major historical events of the twentieth century, belongs in the non-fiction category.

My role as writer was to try to make it possible for the reader to visualise his story. An example: Kamal's love of movie star Doris Day was kindled in the movie theatres of Beirut, and Majda was his 'Doris'. My intervention here as the author, designed to draw the reader in, was to use the song 'My Dreams Are Getting Better All the Time'.

More important still than the question of whether Kamal's account of his life story was truthful is the bigger picture behind it. His personal history is similar to the stories of millions of people who have been robbed of their rights due to their lack of citizenship. The impact this can have on a person's life is enormous and that is what I have tried to capture in this book.

Thanks to Ingrid Halbritter, who introduced me to Kamal. She pointed out the bigger picture behind his story and the importance of writing about it. Thanks also to Paul den Hartog, who travelled to Sarajevo with me and helped me believe in my ability to write the book. I also owe a debt of gratitude to Esmeralda, who gave me the space to keep working on this book.

Thank you to Marieke Wegman for the German translation of the

Sarajevo chapter and to Ingrid for her helpful comments. Thanks to Franziska Rauber and Zoubeida Ben Salah for interpreting during my interviews with Kamal. Laura van Waas from the Institute on Statelessness and Inclusion provided valuable professional legal feedback on the Sarajevo chapter. I would like to thank Rene Bruin of UNHCR Netherlands for his feedback on the book as a whole, and for his support in my efforts to get this story out there.

Thanks to my co-readers Gonny ten Haaft, Maarten Hidskes, Carolien Duivenvoorde and Job de Haan for their expert feedback and their unflagging interest in my progress.

Finally, I would like thank Judith Koelemeijer, Jan Brokken and Frank Westerman for all they taught me.

BIBLIOGRAPHY

Blagojevic, Slobodan & Demirovic, Hamdija. *De Joegoslavische oorlog en de Europese vrede.* G.A. van Oorschot, 1994

Cicovacki, Borislav. *Wraakengelen, 1500 jaar oorlog op de Balkan.* Atlascontact, 2013

Dedijer, Vladimir. *Jasenovac, het Joegoslavische Ausschwitz en het Vaticaan.* De Geus, 1994

De Tijd, dagblad voor Nederland. *Tsjechische wapenzendingen via Joegoslavië naar Egypte.* 25 January 1956

Glenny, Mischa. *De Balkan 1804-1999.* Kosmos, 2000

Keyrouz, J. *Golden Age of Lebanon 1950-1975* (film). Salibi 2013

Maalouf, Amin. *De ontheemden.* De Geus, 2013

NRC. *Slovenië: massagraven met slachtoffers van Tito.* 10 August 2007

Paris, Edmond. *Genocide in Satellite Croatia, 1941-1945. A Record of Racial and Religious Persecutions and Massacres.* The American Institute for Balkan Affairs, 1961

Rivelli, Marco Aurelio. *Le genocide occulté, état indépendant de Croatie 1941-1945*. Editions, L'age d'Homme, 1998

Saade, C. Chatila, I. *Agricultural Performance and Policy in Lebanon.* Ciheam, 1994

UNHCR Nederland. *Staatloosheid in Nederland.* 2011

United Nations. *Convention on the Reduction of Statelessness 1961.* UNHCR, 2014

United States General Accounting Office. *Humanitarian Intervention. Effectiveness of U.N. Operations in Bosnia.* April 1994

Vlijmen, L. van. *Joegoslavië lijdt aan dollarburgers.* Leidse Courant, 4 April 1980